How to **Live & Do Business in China**

*Eight Lessons I Learned
from the Communists.*

Ernie Tadla

www.odysseychina.net

Trafford
PUBLISHING

Order this book online at www.trafford.com/06-1877
or email orders@trafford.com

Most Trafford titles are also available at major online book retailers.

Note for Librarians: A cataloguing record for this book is available from Library
and Archives Canada at www.collectionscanada.ca/amicus/index-e.html

Printed in Victoria, BC, Canada.

ISBN: 978-1-4251-0120-6

*We at Trafford believe that it is the responsibility of us all, as both individuals
and corporations, to make choices that are environmentally and socially sound.
You, in turn, are supporting this responsible conduct each time you purchase a
Trafford book, or make use of our publishing services. To find out how you are
helping, please visit www.trafford.com/responsiblepublishing.html*

*Our mission is to efficiently provide the world's finest, most comprehensive
book publishing service, enabling every author to experience success.
To find out how to publish your book, your way, and have it available
worldwide, visit us online at www.trafford.com/10510*

www.trafford.com

North America & international
toll-free: 1 888 232 4444 (USA & Canada)
phone: 250 383 6864 ♦ fax: 250 383 6804
email: info@trafford.com

The United Kingdom & Europe
phone: +44 (0)1865 722 113 ♦ local rate: 0845 230 9601
facsimile: +44 (0)1865 722 868 ♦ email: info.uk@trafford.com

10 9 8 7 6 5 4

DEDICATION

This book is dedicated to Dan Mintz and Wu Bing who had the faith to bring me to China to execute an important next phase of their China business.

They were unstinting with their support, encouragement, coaching and patience as I learned from them the Chinese way of doing business (often as a slow learner).

Their generosity and love for me and my wife, Lovy, transformed a business deal into a family relationship that also included a learning, cultural and spiritual aspect.

My life is forever changed by the opportunity they gave me to live and learn in China.

Thank you, Wu Bing and Dan!

Testimonials

Dan Mintz, founder and chief creative officer,
DYNAMIC MARKETING GROUP
www.dmgmedia.com

"Ernie Tadla: Motivator, magician and spiritual guide. Ernie has kept us on track as both our business and corporate culture/ conscience.

"His fair and open approach has allowed our group of companies to grow and prosper in what could be a very complicated international environment. A grower of businesses and a farmer of people, he always makes sure his crops have enough sunlight, water and TLC. He brought a sense of purpose and value/meaning to our organizations. His 25+ years of international business experience and wisdom have been a powerful positive influence on our management, staff and clients."

Daniel Ding, Group Account Director,
ASATSU-DK ADVERTISING CO. LTD.

"For almost five years, Ernie has always been one of my first choices for both business and friendship. His wisdom has contributed largely to my business success, ever since I started talking with him when I was at 3M, then later at GM. Every meeting with him was a meeting of the minds....."

Irv Beiman, PhD, Chairman,
eGate Consulting Shanghai, Ltd.

"Ernie Tadla is a professional who has achieved a unique balance of business knowledge, China experience, life wisdom and individual character. You can trust Ernie to tell you the truth, to give you excellent advice, to work for your optimum benefit, and to help you uncover those blind spots that pose a risk for your business and individual goals."

Michael C.R. Dong, Marketing Director,
Nanjing Iveco (FIAT) Motor Company Ltd.

"In China, more than in anywhere else, before doing any serious business together, you have to build up guanxi. Unlike most Westerners I've met, Ernie has the right "human touch" to deal with Chinese people that most others, who no matter how good they are and how long they've stayed in this country, just don't get."

Luca Mignini, Vice President,
SC Johnson Greater China Cluster

"People who come to work in China quickly realize that this country is more like a continent than a nation. When I landed in Shanghai, I was puzzled by Ernie's depth, knowledge and variety · of China's cultural traditions, which are not always obvious to a foreigner.

"Having the need of focusing first on what was happening inside my company, I looked outside for a senior executive coach who could help me in understanding the Chinese people, Chinese business, someone who had gone through the same adjustment I was going through.

"I met Ernie for the first time over three years ago and our regular meetings are always a unique opening on human nature, business and operational decisions and also, the pleasure of spending some quality time with a special person.

"To get better at whatever we are doing is a journey. This process itself may be as rewarding as achieving a specific goal. I have found Ernie to be an excellent companion and stimulator that makes that an even more interesting quest."

ACKNOWLEDGMENTS

There would be no China story, and no book, without the unconditional love, guidance, and patience of my high-school sweetheart wife of forty-three years, Lovy, who passed away March 2002 from cancer after three of the best years of our lives in Shanghai. She peeled the scales from my prejudiced eyes to see the Chinese people as they really are.

This book would not have been written without the encouragement, inspiration, support, coaching and gentle caring and kindness of Cora Meeks, who came into my life October 2005.

Ross Freake, my editor, guided me through a wonderful transformative process that enabled me to more fully express my thoughts in a much clearer and proper way. Thank you, Ross.

CONTENTS

PART II: THE LESSONS

PART III: CASE STUDIES

    The Conversation That Changed My Life:

    One Man's Spiritual Odyssey.

FOREWORD

Ernie Tadla is a wonderful human being with a story to tell. Actually, he has many stories to tell, and he weaves them together into a tapestry that briefly illuminates the rich complexity of a culture with 5,000 years of history. Ernie is a veteran of China. Those who have achieved such status know what that means. He's more than a survivor; he used the challenges as a springboard for a richer, more meaningful and aware life. Why should that interest us, or you, the reader? Because we learn from the stories that Ernie tells.

I have lived and worked in this fascinating land for almost 15 years. Every story from Ernie rings true to me. They are valid representations of life and work in China. Ernie has, however, gone further than that. He has peered beneath the veil and found depth that few foreigners see or understand. He reports on that depth in a meaningful way, with a good heart, honest intention and a twinkle in his eye.

Ernie tells us of sorrow, of success, of charity, and of Great Learning. I call it Great Learning because it is of a dimension beyond what we normally consider to be learning. This is learning that the businessman with a soul might occasionally experience. Ernie brought his soul to China, and became a better man for it. He tells us of his business, his organization, his family, friends, wives, everything about his journey.

We learn with Ernie as he writes.

Read this book if you want a glimpse behind the veil of what is presented on television and in the print media about China. Read this book if you are considering coming to China. Read this book if you are in China.

It will illuminate your journey!

Irv Beiman, PhD
Chairman, eGate Consulting Shanghai, Ltd.

Part I:

Background & Preparation

CHAPTER ONE
What happened to me while I was writing this book

*"Oh, East is East, and West is West,
and never the twain shall meet,*

*Till Earth and Sky stand presently at
God's great Judgment Seat;*

*But there is neither East nor West,
border, nor breed, nor birth,*

*When two strong men stand face to face,
though they come from the ends of the earth!"*

Rudyard Kipling, 1889

When I went to China, I had a negative, self-righteous view of all things Chinese. It was a communistic, godless dictatorship. We, on the other hand, were a capitalistic, democratic, Christian society.

So after seven years and several major epiphanies, I changed my paradigm and discovered many positive things about the Chinese way.

I returned to Canada and wrote this book from my fresh, new Chinese perspective. My editor, Ross Freake, brought to my attention that I was now bashing the Western way as I had earlier bashed the Chinese way. I had been infected with the Stockholm syndrome. You are now reading a complete revision and change in attitude and paradigm, but not back to what it was before; there would be no gain in that.

Through synchronicity, I received another epiphany.

It is the concept of whole-brain integration.

I came across a book, *PSYCH-K: The Missing Peace in Your Life!* by Robert Williams. On page 41, in the chapter on whole-brain integration he charts some differences between the two brain hemispheres.

The left hemisphere	The right hemisphere
* uses logic/reason	* uses intuition/emotions
* thinks in words	* thinks in pictures
* deals in parts/specifics	* deals in wholes/relationships
* will analyze/break apart	* will synthesize/put together
* thinks sequentially	* thinks holistically
* is time bound	* is time free
* is extroverted	* is introverted
* is characterized as male	* is characterized as female
* identifies with the individual	* identifies with the group
* is ordered/controlled	* is spontaneous/free

Later on page 43, he cites clinical psychologist Ernest Rossi expressing the importance of learning how to create balance with both sides of the brain and he uses a comparison chart.

analysis vs. synthesis

reasoning vs. intuition

extroversion vs. introversion

outer vs. inner

male vs. female

friend vs. enemy

capitalism vs. communism

My a-ha! The West is left-brain and the East is right brain!

Our actual brain structure includes the corpus callosum, a band of nerve fibers that bridges the two hemispheres. Interestingly, the female corpus callosum has 33 per cent more neurons than the male. That leads us to suppose that the female integrates both sides better than the male. Maybe that is why women can multi-task better than us guys.

East, West, left, right, wrong, right: which is best, which is right?

I believe the right way for humanity is to balance, to integrate the best parts of both. Instead of yes-but, it is yes-and.

Might this kind of thinking help us in our desperate search for world peace? Let us build bridges and have harmony, prosperity and peace.

CHAPTER TWO
Apprehension and trepidation

After twenty-five years of management experience with Johnson & Johnson (J&J), Bristol Myers-Squibb and Quadra Logic Technologies, (QLT), I became a "corporate refugee," a middle-aged, middle manager who was downsized in the recession of the '80s. There were thousands of us walking around in a daze. After years of education and successful corporate performance, we were out on the streets.

When you can't get a real job, you become a consultant, which is why I founded Odyssey Consulting International Inc. I was doing for my own stable of clients what I had been doing for my corporate employers.

My corporate management track record consisted of two elements:

I was a people person and had a talent as a change agent. When I graduated, I was hired as a pharmaceutical sales rep for Ortho Pharmaceuticals, a division of Johnson & Johnson. I became the guy they moved from territory to territory to clean up the mess made by a previous sales person, to help launch a new product or to work in the field with new reps.

As I matured in the industry, I began doing this at divisional and regional levels. At QLT Pharmaceuticals, it expanded into a corporate start-up role and in China. Later with PPI and DMG, I made an entrance onto the international stage.

Growing up in the business, I observed there were two kinds

of managers: cops and gardeners. The cops worked with their people by handing out tickets. You did this wrong. You are not supposed to do this; you are to do it this way, my way.

Gardeners focused on the strengths of their people, caught them doing the right things and were more interested in growing their business by growing their staff.

Always an observer of results, I noticed that the gardener managers had less turnover, higher morale, better increases and higher profits.

I aspired and trained to be a gardener. Gardening was easy for me, but I was not a good cop.

Second, I was a change agent, a builder, and a pioneer. Because many people fear and resist change, some called me a shit disturber. So be it. I am a firm believer that if you keep doing what you have always been doing, you will continue to get the same results. If you want different results, better results, then you need to change what you're doing. To me, the change process was not about an external rearranging of the deck chairs, changing the systems, reducing costs and the other superficial techniques we read about.

The change process has three steps.

1. First, change your attitude, your perception of yourself, your job, your customers and your company.

2. When that is embedded, you'll automatically experience a change in behavior.

3. A change in results follows only a change in behavior.

It usually took me two to three years to build, fix or turn around an organization. When I had completed the assignment, the profile of the job changed from builder to operational maintenance. I wasn't a good administrator. I became bored and my boss became impatient because I no longer fit the bill for what he now needed. So I moved on, gaining invaluable experience in another setting, another industry, another corporate culture and now, another country. This was a great asset for a consulting/coaching career or for writing a book.

I had built up this philosophy over the years, after, of course, much trial and error. I learn quickly and well from what does not work. This was my corporate history, my consulting style, and my confidence base.

A good consultant should always be doing himself out of a job.

Scouting and prospecting for new assignments and projects is a constant and important function. I was in that mode when I learned a Chinese TV commercial production house was looking for a contract director of business development.

We were living in Richmond, B.C. — a high density Oriental suburb of Vancouver — and I was active in the Chamber of Commerce. I had worked with Chinese member business people on several committees and knew they were interested in expanding their businesses to the non-Asian business market.

I assumed that the Chinese television commercial production house was Vancouver-based and wanted a gweilo to establish business liaison for them in the gweilo business community in Richmond and Vancouver. In China, foreigners are called foreign devils or gweilos.

Ten years earlier, I had been approached by a headhunter for

QLT, a biotech research company with a separate division in a three-way joint-venture partnership with Lison Chemicals Inc., a Hong Kong company and a Chinese government pharmaceutical company in Guangzhou, Guangdong Province, China. The joint-venture company, QLT Pharmaceutical Inc. was looking for an executive consultant familiar with the pharmaceutical industry in North America to determine the feasibility of establishing a manufacturing plant in British Columbia to produce finished product from Chinese raw material for the North American market.

While conducting my research, I had traveled to China, Hong Kong, South Korea, and Taiwan for three two-week trips. My wife, Lovy, accompanied me on one. This was my first introduction to China in the late '80s. I met and worked with some very capable people. While back in my Vancouver office, I experienced great difficulty, frustration and exasperation communicating with my Chinese contacts and getting them to do what they had promised me.

I remember thinking, "What's going on here? We're partners; we have a common goal. Why the foot dragging, the delays?"

But in spite of my frustration, the QLT Pharmaceuticals board in Guangzhou, China, unanimously accepted my report and I was hired, as the first employee, to implement it.

The plum of this joint venture was to be able to establish a finished goods manufacturing plant in Vancouver. Dr. Jim Miller, one of the founders and CEO of QLT, was ready to use this as a fundraiser for government money. However, my research and report did not recommend this as a feasible idea. The market was on the East coast.

I found that with the powerful alliances with the Hong Kong and Chinese partners that to develop a market for Chinese bulk vitamins and other over-the-counter products was a feasible plan.

Two events eventually forced QLT to end the joint venture, and my contract. The major investor, Cyanamid, a U.S. company, wanted QLT to focus on its photodynamic cancer therapy product, and at the same time the Tiananmen Square episode caused a rupture between China and the rest of the world, making business and joint ventures difficult and touchy.

I had learned much during those years and developed a great respect for what China was doing and wanted to do as it was opening up to the West.

Tiananmen Square and the approaching date of when Hong Kong would be handed over to China caused a tidal wave of immigration to the Vancouver area. While many Richmondites grumbled and complained about the Chinese invasion, I was impressed with what they brought to our community, even though they were from Hong Kong and Taiwan, not Mainland China. I enjoyed and respected their hard work, their drive, their wealth, their ambition and the studiousness of their children.

They loved Richmond because it was close to the airport and they often flew home. Every thing has meaning to the Chinese. Richmond, with its reference to "rich," also made settling there attractive. In the twenty-five years we lived in Richmond, we saw the ratio go from fifteen per cent to sixty five per cent Oriental mix. I know what it feels like to live in Canada and be a member of a visible minority.

I was interested in an opportunity to work more closely with this new, burgeoning community and felt that they could learn from me about Western and British Columbia business and business practices. I believed I could make a solid contribution to their Asian business in B.C.

My first contact with my soon-to-be employer was a fellow Canadian, Paul Van Dergarten, who had just spent five years working for Dan Mintz in Shanghai. Paul missed the mountains, skiing and fresh air and wanted to return home. Dan asked him to find his replacement when he returned home. Dan, from New York City via Los Angeles, liked working with Canadians. We didn't have Hollywood-sized egos and the exchange rate made it attractive for a Canadian who would be paid in U.S. dollars.

At our first meeting, I discovered the position was not in Vancouver, but in Beijing and Shanghai. Realizing that this was not what I had expected, (I am quite transparent) Paul asked if I was still interested in the project.

"No," I said.

"Tadla, why are you saying no?" my other self asked.

"I am saying no because I do not speak Chinese." I told my other self and Paul at the same time.

Paul said I could learn to speak Chinese if I wished, but since I would be dealing with marketing directors of foreign multinational firms, it wasn't a requirement and wouldn't affect my performance.

Even though he was still talking, Paul faded into the background as I was frozen by a blizzard of thoughts. Things were happening quickly. Move to China? Leave everything? What would Lovy say? I needed to sleep on this. But my gut, intuition and other self barked, "Go for it, Ern!"

We had established good rapport. We made arrangements to have lunch the next day at TGIF on Robson Street in Vancouver. Thank God It's Friday (TGIF) was his favorite place in Beijing and Shanghai, as it would later also become mine.

"What do you think about me taking an assignment in China?" I asked Lovy when I returned home after the first meeting.

"Well, we don't have a cat or a dog, the kids are on their own, let's go!" she said.

The magic of many marriages, friendships, partnerships, and alliances is when two parties of different, almost opposite views and talents can accept their differences and work together, complementing each other bringing synergy and power to the union. Such was the differences between Lovy and I. She was steadfast, practical, levelheaded, the stabilizing factor of our marriage. I was the dreamer, the idea person, and the big picture guy. She worked for the same boss for twenty-seven years. I changed bosses every two to three years. When she said, "Let's go!" in what seemed a role reversal, I understood perfectly.

Four years earlier, Lovy had been diagnosed with terminal kidney disease. Both kidneys had shut down and she had been on dialysis for two years, which we both knew was not a long-term solution. Our son, Dana, donated one of his kidneys and gave his mother an extended and new lease on life and living. Having stared death in the face, she had started living with a new zest. She had been granted an extension and she was going to take full advantage of it. Even at that point, we were aware that a kidney transplant also has a limited lifespan, seven to eight years. But she had undergone a personal transformation. We now knew life was short, unpredictable and uncertain.

Life is for living. It was this attitude of hers that made those three years together in China the best of our forty-three years of marriage.

I was sixty-one years old, with 40 years of Canadian pharmaceutical sales, marketing, management and training experience. Sort of been, there done that, wore out the T-shirt. The independent consulting business was slow and sporadic. It seemed like the timing of a China adventure with a New York/Los Angeles entrepreneur in the film production business was a good next step for us.

Lovy had started packing.

That was fine for Lovy, new lease, new life and all.

While she was packing, I was wrestling with my other self.

To change jobs, bosses, companies and move to Ottawa, Toronto, Edmonton, and Vancouver were OK. Change and variety motivate me, but this was different. To move to another country when I didn't know the language, the culture, or the industry and work for a small, independent entrepreneurial company with a mercurial, New York Jewish boss, was different.

My initial eagerness was being tempered now with self-doubt and second-guessing. Lovy was ready! Was I?

I want to address the issue of self-talk. It goes by many names. Essentially, it's called thinking, the inner dialogue we all carry on within ourselves. Some call it ego or conscience; to some it is right brain/left brain chatter, your positive self vs. your negative self. Back in the 1960s, Paul Meyer, who founded Success Motivation Institute in Waco, Texas, used this concept as affirmations.

While most of us entertain self-talk on a more or less random basis, depending on our reactions, moods, and upbringing,

Meyer's affirmations were deliberate, intentional statements about what it was that you desired. Statements were in the first person and in the present tense.

The dialogue below was just my ponderings on what I should do. As usual, the emotional/heart, right brain response is always positive, trusting, forward moving. The other side, the intellectual, rational, left-brain, chatter is logical, fearful and doubt driven. That's why I initially was for this, and now was hearing from my other side. I had to entertain and answer these questions because others would ask them.

> "Wait a minute, Ern. Just pick up and go to China? What about your business here, your contacts, the people who know you, your family, the comforts and knowing your Canadian culture? Leave that behind? "Have you thought about this, the ramifications? You're not a young man who can bounce at all, never mind bounce back, if it doesn't work out. What do you know about China? Have you been reading the papers? It's a godless, communistic dictatorship without respect for human rights. You have no idea what they can do to short, stocky gweilos."

Then, there was:

> "What do you know about TV commercial production and selling this to marketing directors of global multinational companies in Canada, let alone in China?"

Followed by:

> "And what about your new boss? The guy you're trusting with your wife's and your present and future. Your preliminary due diligence and intuition tell you he is a young, typical New York entrepreneur: edgy, high energy, quick paced, impatient, controlling and demanding. He will chew you up and ship you back as soon as he finds out your weaknesses and all the stuff you don't know and have never done. Are you out of your mind? Go back and do some more networking at the Richmond Chamber of Commerce meetings. You're good at that. People know you. They like you. Get some business there!"

There were no such questions from Lovy. She believed in me and knew that there was more for me than I was then involved with. My normally practical, common sense wife felt, intuitively, that this was good for us. She was ready. She was right!

Like her rebirth after her kidney transplant, this opportunity also held too much appeal, mystery and adventure for me. How could I not take advantage of this? I couldn't spend the rest of my 20 plus years here wondering what we might have missed. Lovy's experience had taught me what we all know: Life is great, but unpredictable and impermanent. Carpe diem!

"Without uncertainty and the unknown ...you become the victim of the past, and your tormentor today is your self left over from yesterday," author Deepak Chopra wrote.

I left for Beijing with trepidation, apprehension and excitement.

Chapter Three
First impressions

So the gweilo got on an Air China flight.

It seems I was the only non-Chinese person on the plane.

The culture shock began there. Flying Air China is not like flying Air Canada. We take our western comforts for granted and don't really appreciate what we have until it's taken away. This was a good, gradual first phase introduction for me. Take all we are used to here and knock it down three notches. Space, service, quality whether washrooms, seating, or food. I did not suffer, but realized that I was like a city guy going to visit country cousins on the farm. I was going from a developed society to a developing society. They were trying to catch up with us, and doing a great job, but were not there yet.

Alone with my thoughts, I wondered and worried. What was I getting myself into? The pangs of being alone were deep. It would be four months before Lovy would join me. Without her at my side, I was at the mercy of others and my own mental meanderings. Would Dan and his partners, Wu Bing and Peter, accept me? Would the Chinese staff accept me? How would I order things since I didn't know the language? Would I succeed? How would I begin? What would I do?

Then the "what ifs" started. What if they don't accept me? What if I don't succeed? What if? What if?

Then, as always, I fell back on my foundation blocks.

Number one: my strong, deep, spiritual roots and beliefs that there is a Higher Power of Infinite Intelligence. It had brought me through sixty years of highs and lows and was not going to abandon me now.

Number two: my whole life has been a journey of new beginnings, opening new territories, introducing new products, starting new divisions, being a pioneer, going where few or none had gone before.

This was my destiny. I was good at it. This had been my whole life.

I had the same doubts and fears before each new adventure and experienced the quiet self-satisfaction of getting the job done while remaining authentic to my values, purpose and beliefs.

"Lighten up, Ern," I told myself. "Enjoy. Believe. Have faith. Remember your past successes. What happened then will happen again, in China."

Living in Richmond for twenty-seven years and my Asian experience with QLT had prepared me for this adventure. Lovy's newfound zest for life after her kidney transplant provided me with the back-up support and steadying influence I needed. The Richmond Chinese shopping malls and dining emporiums were also good preparation.

A distinction should be made here. Most Chinese people in Vancouver and Richmond were Cantonese from Hong Kong. While they are Chinese and Hong Kong is now part of China, politically, there is a cultural gap between Hong Kong Chinese (population, seven million) and Mainland Chinese (population, 1.3 billion) as pronounced as there is between the East and West. Chinese people from Hong Kong and Guangzhou speak Cantonese. In Beijing and Shanghai, Mandarin is the spoken language, although each city has its own dialect, as well as cuisine.

I deplaned at the Beijing Capital International Airport about 8 p.m. The airport was what you would expect for a city of twenty million people and the capital of China. It was new, impressive and packed with wall-to-wall people. I was swept up in the flow of the crowd and found myself at the arrivals location. The lights were bright and the crowd noisy.

It seemed that a group of people talking Chinese made more noise than a group of people talking English. O'Hare in Chicago, the busiest airport in the U.S., seemed uncrowded and quiet in comparison. The Vancouver airport similarly seemed silent and empty.

Someone in the sea of people awaiting arriving passengers was holding up a sign with ERNIE TADLA. PPI. What a welcome sight. The forty-minute drive to the PPI office was quiet, no idle conversation due to my lack of Chinese and his lack of English. I gawked at the night scenes, lights, and traffic, and the tension built, as we got closer to the office.

Dan and his partners, Wu Bing and Peter Xiao, met me, warmly.

The Beijing PPI office was off the main street, down a lane and was an eclectic blend of Chinese design, L.A. flare and an expected film industry atmosphere. The building had been constructed around two large trees, to protect them from destruction. It was 9 p.m., but the office was busy with animated people yelling to each other.

The Chinese reputation for hard work is well earned. They work six and a half days a week, putting in twelve to eighteen hour days, often working into the wee hours of the morning. This was not a slave labor camp. Many staff are from the countryside and live alone in small, simple accommodation. The office community provided them with space, bright lights, camaraderie, social interaction, friendship and excitement. Sometimes, even romance. Each company must provide a staff kitchen and cook.

Dan and Wu Bing took me to inspect my new apartment, my home for the next three months. It was nicely furnished in a non-Canadian way. Everything was new and strange, but I approved. They seemed relieved.

The next day I was introduced to Helen (English name), who would be the first of several intelligent, quick, English-speaking Chinese ladies who would be my executive assistants. They provided for my survival, not only doing my administrative work and translating, but guiding me in dealing with the Chinese staff. Helen was pretty, smart and friendly, and originally from Inner Mongolia.

The original plan was that Lovy would join me after my ninety-day probationary period was over and I had moved to Shanghai. Dan was then to leave for Los Angeles where he would begin producing and directing his first feature length movie Cookers, for the U.S. market.

Before Dan left for LA. he had me draw an Osho Zen Tarot card from his deck. I drew The Fool. The interpretation read:

> "Moment to moment, and with every step, the Fool
> leaves the past behind. He carries nothing more than
> his purity, innocence and trust. At this moment, the
> Fool has the support of the universe to make this

jump into the unknown. Adventures await him in the river of life. Your actions may appear 'foolish' to others, or even to yourself, if you try to analyze them with the rational mind. But you are in the place where trust and innocence are the guides, not skepticism and past experiences."

I had never heard of Osho Zen Tarot cards before. My boss, who I had questions and fears about, the whole China excursion, all my previous inner talks and questions were swept away by the obvious glee Dan and Wu Bing showed when I drew my card. Up until then, I had been a closet spiritualist, particularly with this hard-driving, hard-nosed New York entrepreneur. This was the beginning of an additional level to our relationship, a wonderful, rich alliance, strictly business, but also a deep friendship with Lovy and me, which extended to the spiritual level. They were also on a journey, an odyssey, as it were, looking for more than material success and the glitzy glamour of the entertainment world. Several times before I left for Shanghai, they took me to a fantastic Buddhist retreat north of Beijing, a hallowed place where we experienced a traditional tea ceremony, talked into the night, meditated and replenished our souls together.

When Lovy arrived, she and Wu Bing immediately hit it off. We were quite the team, all so different and yet connected so deeply in the next phase of our journeys. Even then we knew this was not a long-term deal, but we were there to make the best of it during the time allotted. And we did.

When Lovy and I celebrated our 40th anniversary, I wanted to celebrate it at the Buddhist retreat, but foreigners couldn't get reservations because it was close to a Peoples' Liberation Army base.

Funny how I had to come to godless China to find the next step in my spiritual growth. I read further on The Fool card I had drawn.

> "Be a fool in the Taoist sense, in the Zen sense. Don't try to create a wall of knowledge around you. Whatsoever experience comes to you let it happen, and then go on dropping it. Go on cleaning your mind continuously; go on dying to the past so you remain in the present, as if just born, just a babe. Your soul will become more crystallized."

The Perfect Universe was unfolding just as it must. I was in the right place at the right time. All was well. An earlier mentor told me that whenever I came to a cross in the road, one path would be easy and one more difficult. The difficult, less-traveled road would be where all the prizes were. Let the adventure continue.

OK, enough of that stuff, now, back to business. Dan and Wu Bing were working sixteen to eighteen hour days. Dan was a typically dedicated entrepreneur, committed and devoted to building his business, driving and bringing his staff along with him. I was left to fend for myself and make my own arrangements. Anything I asked for or asked about was quickly and efficiently provided. But I had to ask. I was in a totally hands-off situation.

Now, for the first time in forty years, I was without my Lovy. I missed her dearly. I was alone in a strange country, a super-charged work atmosphere, without language and therefore communication ability. This was unlike anything I had ever experienced. I really missed Lovy around meal times. I was a past generation husband with no cooking, laundry, or ironing skills.

So, my first morning in Beijing, I woke up with food on my mind.

I ventured out onto the busy street. I noticed breakfast stalls, with people ordering, leaving, or sitting at makeshift tables and chairs. I watched. It smelled great and looked good. I edged up the stall and hesitantly pointed to what I wanted. Since I'm not sure how to handle the chopsticks, I ordered a wonton soup-like dish. Later, I ordered a great smelling and looking flap of fried dough with egg, a layer of filling, plus spices, etc. It was delicious and then I walked to the office.

This was quickly followed by my initiation rites into a new culture — the Yellow Emperor's revenge. My digestive system was not familiar with the new flora and fauna of this strange place. It responded in typical expected fashion. For weeks, I lived with the most horrific case of diarrhea. In anticipation, I had brought Imodium, but it was ineffective. I suffered horribly until I figured out two things.

1. Don't eat at the street stalls. The food smelled great and tasted wonderfully. Everyone else was eating it. I wasn't concerned about hygiene, but maybe I should have been. There certainly were no food inspectors visible.

2. Before leaving Canada, my doctor gave me three only capsules of the powerful antibiotic, Cipro, the drug of choice in the U.S. during the anthrax scare after 9/11. Cipro can knock out your e.coli bacteria and/or anthrax often with one dose. Repeated, unmonitored usage probably has the potential to knock out your kidneys, and liver as well.

In China, you can get any prescription drug available in North America without a prescription. So, I was able to carry an ample supply of Cipro at all times. The misery of severe, long-term diarrhea and its urgency took priority over any possible future long-term damage to my kidneys or liver. I would worry about my kidneys tomorrow; today I needed to know where the nearest toilet was. With Lovy carrying one of his kidneys, maybe Dana would be willing to share half of his remaining kidney with his ex-Cipro Dad.

The beauty of life is that everything passes. Eventually, the diarrhea passed. I then learned that I had earned entrance into that group of foreigners who survived this rite of passage. I had earned my stripes. My stomach lining was now aligned with the local Communist Chinese bacteria and other assorted creatures.

I found the Chinese people, both at PPI and on the streets, friendly, warm, smiling, and helpful. Again, as in Richmond, only more so, I was a visible minority. Whenever I spotted a foreigner, I asked, "Where are you from?" I looked forward to talking with another English-speaking person. But often they were from Germany or France and didn't speak English.

PPI was a member of the American Chamber of Commerce-Beijing and I attended their meetings for the three months I lived there. The members had difficulty believing the economic growth figures the Chinese government was posting. Actually, the Chinese government often understated the numbers because they understood that these would be challenging to other governments in the Western world.

Beijing is the political and cultural center of China while Shanghai is the financial and business center. You can compare this to Washington, D.C. and New York City or Ottawa and Toronto. All the foreign embassies are in Beijing with consulates in Shanghai.

Beijing residents are hard working, friendly and helpful to strangers. They're a happy people, but also serious and sincere.

Shanghai is different. The minute I stepped off the plane, I felt the rhythm, the energy. It was throbbing, dynamic, and full of hustle and bustle. Everything moved faster. The same sense you feel between Ottawa and Toronto or Washington, D.C., and New York. I never experienced entrepreneurialism and capitalism to the degree I did in Shanghai and China in general. Even though it's China's largest city — population twenty million — it seems to be all stores. There were blocks and blocks of small, family-run businesses with sleeping and eating quarters behind the store. Because of the high level of entrepreneurialism in Shanghai, you have to be careful dealing with some small shop owners when negotiating (everything is negotiated, except in retail stores) and receiving change — something you never had to do in Beijing. Some will take advantage of the awkward gweilos. Their feeling was that they couldn't trust the foreigners, so why not take advantage of them first?

There was brashness in the air, a sense that all things were possible. Shanghainese have a character of their own. There was a we-them feeling. Shanghainese business people are sharper than anywhere else in China. The women are beautiful, snappy, confident, sharp, directed and vibrant. It is something in the air. Shanghainese have an attitude; a positive, self-confident attitude.

Shanghai is a coastal city 2,100 miles southeast of Beijing and is therefore much warmer, almost tropical.

Because many of our clients were U.S. companies I became active in the American Chamber of Commerce-Shanghai (AM-CHAM). The Chamber was a robust and dynamic business-networking hub for over two thousand American companies providing a complete package of services for U.S. companies in Shanghai. It had 1,400 company members and 3,400 individual members, adding 80 members a month.

AMCHAM-Shanghai was a powerful base for me. As anything in life, you get out of it what you put into it. I got involved and participated across the board. Among the services provided members:

- they lobby the Chinese government on behalf of U.S. business interests in China;

- help you stay informed on Chinese in China. China veterans share their experiences via speeches, panel discussions, committee events;

- a full spectrum general business and industry specific training for yourself and you staff through conferences, workshops, training sessions, speaker events;

- an exposure to high level executives from the U.S. visiting their company plus high ranking government officials from Washington D.C. who were always invited to speak to us at a luncheon or dinner meeting;

- network with your peers through working on 19 committees ranging from manufacturing, marketing, transportation and taxes. I took an active role on the marketing committee and later the training and education committee. I was also asked to serve on the ethics committee vetting members who stood for election to the board of governors;

- on-line job recruiting;

- network with clients at any of 250 events a year. I took advantage to promote PPI and DMG by staging several well-attended events on

  o TV commercial creative design

  o the production process

  o what to look for in selecting an advertising agency

  o what to look for in selecting a PR/events management company

- through the above events I was asked to conduct in-house presentations at companies like GM, SC Johnson, J. Walter Thompson, Ogilvy PR, Gallup, 3M, The American Management Association-Shanghai (AMA).

- closed monthly briefings by the U.S. consulate general.

AMCHAM was a fantastic support and resource in helping me get established. The networking with other English-speaking people from the U.S. was a source of familiarity and strength. The caliber of people was outstanding, and I remain friends and in close contact with some of them.

AMCHAM-Beijing had a different culture than AMCHAM-Shanghai due to the city profile. Shanghai was more member active, having more events in a week than Beijing would have in a month. With Beijing being the capital and Shanghai the business center, this was reflected in the membership, their interests, and activity expectations.

My lifestyle was different from the folks with global multinational companies on an ex-pat package. I lived and worked in the city's hinterland with the common folk. While I say I worked for a U.S. company, the only thing American about it was the founder and creative chief and he was in the U.S. All the rest were Chinese. This was the secret of his success. He understood, accepted, and had assimilated the Chinese way. He is perfectly fluent in Mandarin and even had the thought processes of the Chinese.

I also joined the Shanghai Rotary Club. It was an underground operation, not officially recognized by the Chinese government. The government does not recognize any non-business organization that takes its orders from outside China. The same applies to the Roman Catholic Church.

We had a lively and robust group and I enjoyed the networking, friendliness, and fellowship of our weekly meetings. I have many fond memories of my Rotary in Shanghai experience.

Lovy joined me in July. We were the only gweilos in our district of a few million Chinese people. She dove into the local environs, doing her shopping with the street people and in the wet-markets, using her smile and non-Chinese body language skills. Being a gweilo made her a target of any sharpshooter stall owner when it came to negotiating for her groceries. However, other Chinese ladies and men hovered over her, curious about what the gweilo lady was buying and they would raise a storm when a storeowner cheated her. Such is the warmth and sensitivity to foreigners away from the centers.

In China, everything is possible and negotiable. They begin by quoting a high price; you offer a low price and then the game seesaws back and forth until you both arrive at an acceptable figure. I had to learn how to start the bidding low enough. I invariably started too high from the bottom. Sometimes, when I was in a hurry, I felt I didn't have time to bargain. Since the opening price was acceptable, being much lower than I would have paid at home, I would quickly agree to pay the initial asking price. The shop-owner would have a disappointed look in his eye. I thought he should be glad I paid his top, un-negotiated price. No, he missed the fun of bargaining. It's a ritual and social skill making buying and selling interesting and exciting.

For the Chinese, there is much conversational palaver that goes with the give-and-take. Reasons for giving a better deal range from how large a family they feed (uncles, aunts, grandparents) to how influential and large their network is that they can bring so much more business to them, if they give you a good deal. For me, without knowing Chinese I had to rely on my hand-held calculator or writing my price in ink on my palm.

China was fun and I was glad we came.

Chapter Four
About Lovy

Lovy and I were high-school sweethearts and were married for forty-three years before her untimely death. She had worked and put me through university and contributed mightily to the financial stores of our maturing family. This adventure allowed her the opportunity to retire from being a certified dental assistant and enjoy a totally new life, and China, which she did.

Lovy Catherine Edinger was her official birth name. Her father, Phil always wanted a daughter with that name. Of course, her name always got attention. Imagine sitting in your dentist's chair receiving your regular check-up and the dentist says to his assistant, "Lovy, please pass the suction tube." What thoughts would go through your mind? At work, Lovy was called Lee.

When at a party or shopping in a crowd, instead of me calling her name out loud, we had a signature call, "Yoo hoo" that she responded to, knowing I was looking for her.

When we met new people who reacted to her name, I would suggest that it was her name that was an important factor in our long-term, stable and happy marriage. In any normal relationships, there are times of anger and frustration as was in ours. I found it difficult to maintain my self-righteousness and expound when I, in anger called out her name, "Lovy, you always......blah, blah" Having to say Lovy took the wind out of my sails.

She immersed herself into the city and culture. She supported me in my new position and attended all company and client functions with her customary charm and grace. Everyone loved her.

She took up Chinese watercolor painting. When she completed a painting, she signed it Jade. She relished shopping and negotiating in the local markets. She loved everything Chinese: the city, the people, the goods, the customs, and the habits.

One evening, after returning from the office around 8 p.m., I was doing my daily tirade: pacing back and forth, ranting about how stupid and backward they were. Lovy was always a good listener. Not this day.

She put down the book she was reading and placed her hands carefully in her lap. There was a calmness about her, as if she had been preparing for this moment. She had learned well the lessons that terminal kidney disease and a kidney from your son teaches. These were lessons of life and death. Now was the time to confront this loose cannon before her, yelping about the way the Chinese people were. This was time for some straight talk for and to her man.

"It seems to me like you are getting ready to return home," she said in an icy voice, blue eyes flashing.

I stopped pacing, incredulous. "Return home? Why? This is a great opportunity, an exciting place, a wonderful job and company. What are you talking about?"

"I listen to you every day when you come home talking about how difficult it is to work with the Chinese." Then, stabbing her finger into my face, she delivered the knockout punch:

"Listen! These people have been here for five thousand years and they aren't going to change for you any more than we changed for them when they came to Richmond. If you can't understand

and accept them, let's pack up and go home now because I don't want to listen to this every night for the next two years."

I stopped as if I had walked into a brick wall.

No sympathizing, understanding, empathizing. No "There, there sweetheart. Yes, those Chinese are such terrible people and you are fighting such tremendous obstacles. Poor dear."

I was struck by the practical realism of her statements. I needed that jolt. It did the trick. It was my wake-up call. I will expand on this in my Lessons to follow.

She actually led the way because now she got involved with the people I was complaining about. She was going to demonstrate the Lovy way.

At PPI, with the exception of my assistant, Vivian Sheng, and Ray Tao, the office manager, no one spoke English. The rest of the staff wanted to be able to communicate with Lovy and me. They asked the Chinese management if the company would provide English lessons. When Lovy found out, she volunteered to undertake the assignment, no charge. Without any experience or training, she was confident in herself and wanted to be of service to these wonderful people. They loved it.

They loved her.

One day, Ray Tao told me he had a teaching job for Lovy during the Chinese New Year Festival break in February. A former classmate was the head of a school in Turpan on the Old Silk Road way up in Northwestern China. Turpan, close to the Russian border, is in the heart of the Chinese oil fields and had a large school complex, which looks after the needs of the children of the oilfield workers, including the children of professional foreigners working there. Ray's friend needed a native English teacher to teach the Chinese English teachers. When you learn English from a Chinese teacher, you speak Chinglish. You have the words right, but use the Chinese way of expression and phrasing. So, native English speakers are in demand as teachers regardless of their teaching credentials or experience.

I told Ray that she couldn't go because we had planned our annual trip back to Canada for the same Festival period. Ray said too bad, maybe next time. I never gave it another thought.

Then, one evening, while having dinner on our balcony, I remembered and told Lovy. Lovy was a lovely, private, quiet, smart, sophisticated, lady. Her name was very apt. Always observing, always thinking, but never in center stage, where I like to be. We are so well suited for each other, balancing and complementing each other's strengths. When the full impact of my casual comment hit her, did she ever step out of role.

"You turned down an assignment for me?"

"Well, yes, but you couldn't make it because we're going home to see the kids for our annual leave," I replied, quivering a bit.

"Excuse me, but I will be the one who decides where I will go and what I will do!"

I started to suck wind and began defending my stupidity.

"But Lovy, do you know where Turpan is and what it takes to get there? Seven hours by plane, eleven hours by overnight train in the coldest time and spot in China?"

"I know cold weather. I was born in Saskatchewan, remember. We have lived in Alberta and Ontario. I can handle winter and cold weather. Just dress warm."

"Lovy, I cannot go with you, I am sorry, because I have some important business appointments in Vancouver."

"That's fine. I will go by myself."

"Lovy, you are going up into the boonies of China. You have only one kidney. God only knows what kind of medical facilities and treatment they have up there!"

"I am peeing just fine, thank you very much. I am going.

"I will call Ray tomorrow."

Some of the cold air from Xinjiang Province swept through my heart. It was a rather chilly dinner also.

I went to Canada. She went to Turpan and had the experience of her life. Picture this. My Lovy, one kidney, no teaching certificate, boarded a plane alone in Shanghai for a seven-hour flight into the northern hinterland of China. She bought and took a heater with her. She was met at the airport in Urimuqi by a male stranger who traveled with her by train for another eleven hours, sharing a compartment as the train trundled along in the dark, cold Chinese winter night. She arrived in a strange, cold place, and pulled off another of several feats of her life in China. She was feted by the community, wined and dined by dignitaries, civic and scholastic people, written about and photographed in the local paper. She was invited into their homes and experienced real, authentic Chinese families, homes and hospitality. The students, Chinese English teachers, loved her.

When she returned, her reputation grew and she was invited to teach English to Chinese staff in several multinational companies, doing one-on-one coaching with senior Chinese executives and children in a private school for wealthy parents. She couldn't keep up and had to turn business away.

Through my involvement at AMCHAM, we had formed a circle of friends that constituted several couples, mostly American ex-pat men and their younger, successful Chinese wives. We met weekly for dinners and rotated weekend parties. The families had ayis (eye ee, a Chinese maid) who did the cooking and cleaning as the wives led busy lives in the international business community. Our friends were an eclectic group of outstanding, interesting, warm, friendly, happy people.

There was Irv Beiman and his wife, YongLing Sun, both with PhDs. They met in the U.S. YongLing persuaded Irv to come to China and start a business in Shanghai, the first management consulting company serving the U.S. business community. Hewitt Associates, the largest HR firm in the world, bought them out and they retired to Maui. But they missed the dynamic environment in Shanghai and returned a year later to start another flourishing firm providing strategic management systems consulting along with introducing the Balanced Scorecard concept to China.

There was Marjorie Woo, who was born in Taiwan, grew up in Shanghai, and was educated in the U.S. She had a successful track record with Xerox in the U.S., transferred to Shanghai and then started her own company, Keystone Leadership with a master franchise for all of China with LMI, a management leadership training firm. This was the same firm, whose SMI course I had taken 35 years earlier in Canada. I met Marjorie at the first Chamber Marketing Committee meeting I attended during my first week in Shanghai. Marjorie and Lovy became close friends. When Lovy knew she would die soon, she asked Marjorie to "keep an eye on me," which she did. Lovy knew that I would be a basket case without her. She was right. That is partly why I married a Chinese lady seventeen months after her death.

There was Rick Foristel, China executive director for the Webster University MBA programs in China. Then, he was squiring around a revolving bevy of Chinese lovelies, but is now settled, and married to a Chinese senior executive with an American bank.

Keke was another rising star with Xerox who started her own consulting firm. Her husband, Tom, an Australian was a brilliant PhD with HP.

Ari was the GM of a global Dutch chemical company. His Chinese wife, Vivienne, was with the Swedish telecom company Eriksson.

Hugo was a Dutch international lawyer while his Korean wife, Rana, was a designer and art promoter.

All these people were active AMCHAM people: smart, hardworking, popular and recognized as leaders in the Shanghai American business community.

Whether it is was her Chinglish clients, my staff at PPI and DMG, our ex-pat friends or the young Chinese student from down the hall who exchanged English for Chinese lessons with her, Lovy was the magic that attracted the love, respect and admiration from all and the glue that held us all together. Of course, she was my strongest asset.

When 9/11 occurred, the Americans were in a state of shock, pain and concern for their families and friends back home. The following day, I received a phone call from Marjorie asking if they could all meet at our apartment. Even though we were Canadians, they felt a sense of peace, quiet strength, love and harmony at the home that Lovy had created. They just wanted to meet, support each other, heal, and feel comforted in an atmosphere of peace and love. When they came, they also brought other close friends, who felt so lost and alone from this awesome shock. Such was the environment Lovy presented to our ex-pat friends and family.

When Lovy passed on in March, 2002, we had a Celebration of Life for her in Cultus Lake, B.C., where she had bought a retirement home for us. Dan Mintz, who was busy in Los Angeles with the production of his feature movie, fly to Vancouver, drove to Chilliwack and spent several days with me and our family. He delivered a wonderful glimpse of his impressions of her complete with photographs of her, his staff, and us at PPI functions.

CHAPTER FIVE

- ◆ Church in the Park
- ◆ Beggar on the Street

Church in the Park

We lived in a lovely, spacious apartment in a complex of four buildings a block from the PPI studios. We were the only foreigners in the area, so we stood out. The local people were friendly and the guards at the gate were always helpful. We had two bedrooms, one of which became Lovy's office, two baths, a Chinese kitchen, dining room and living room. We lived on the fourth floor and our balcony overlooked a busy intersection that provided much entertainment. We enjoyed late night dinners on the balcony watching the evening parade of humanity below. It was always busy, always changing depending on the time of day or the season.

Just across the street from the office was Zhongshan Park, an oasis in the middle of the busy, throbbing, and noisy section of the city. It was over six square city blocks with heavy tropical foliage, pools, canals, Chinese rock gardens, bridges, fields for kite-flying, benches and lots of open areas of grass. During weekends, it was crowded with families with children and grandparents. Taking pictures of the children was the most predominant activity. The children played and flew kites with their fathers and grandfathers. It was a crowded, happy place. During weekday afternoons, it was almost deserted and was peaceful and quiet. This time and atmosphere also attracted lovers of all ages who sat on the benches, enjoying each other in the most proper fashion.

I often get up at 4 a.m., and as the day wears on, so do I. Between 1-2 p.m., I would slip out, cross the street to the park, lie down on a bench and have a power nap, meditation, snooze, relax, call it what you will. Ten minutes and my batteries were re-charged, as if I had another four hours sleep, and I could continue to work until 8 p.m. I would put my glasses on the bench just above my head. One day, when I got up, the glasses were gone. Someone had stolen them.

Several days later, I was approached in the park by a chap who offered to sell my glasses back to me. We played the game of Chinese negotiation. I had paid 1,500 RMB ($180 US) for them at a Shanghai optometry store. He wanted 500 ($60 US). After several rounds of play, I bought them back for 50 ($6 US). Without speaking a word to each other, with a smile on his face, my face, we good naturedly, with my pocket calculator, haggled. Getting angry and yelling at him in English would not have accomplished anything. I recovered my prescription glasses and investment for an additional $6 along with this story to share with you. The $180 I originally paid was still a fifth of what I would have paid back home. I will repeat: Chinese negotiation is a game, a win/win fun game — even if it is buying back what was stolen from you. Wouldn't that be great if we could do that if our valuables are stolen from us here in North America? To recover my prescription glasses for $6 was a steal.

I took every opportunity to walk for my exercise. While dodging and weaving along the busy sidewalks, I would vocalize my daily affirmations in a loud voice. Just so you know, Oprah, Wayne Dyer, and many other people practice affirmations and visualization. This is different from talking with your "other self." I was the only gweilo around, no one knew me, and they didn't understand what I was saying. Sure, I drew curious looks, but that happened anyway.

One day, as I was marching down a busy street vocalizing my affirmations I got a call on my cell from Ray, our office manager. He sounded concerned and asked if I was OK. Someone had seen me talking loudly to myself and phoned the office. I guess they thought the crazy gweilo needed medical attention.

Often, while I was walking, I would suddenly gain a companion, usually a young, male university student who wanted to practice English with a native English speaker.

One morning, about 6 a.m. I wandered over to the park and was astounded to see crowds of people streaming into the front entrance of Zhongshang Park. I had previously used the back entrance on my way to my power nap and scene of the crime of my stolen glasses. They were:

- doing tai chi, of course

- doing Chinese sword dance

- the scarf dance

- doing ballroom dancing, with their ghetto blasters

- playing cards

- just chatting with friends

- flying kits

- older men with bird cages giving their birds the morning air

- standing in the trees

- meditating in the trees

- praying in the trees

- hugging trees

- talking to the trees

They were all doing their own thing. Morning after morning, every morning. Their actions, whatever they were, had a "spiritual sense" about them.

I began taking my morning walk in the park because the energy felt so good. The same scene, from 6-8 a.m., took place in every park in every city in China. It was repeated wherever there was space for fifteen to forty people to gather. There was always a tape deck playing quiet, flowing, and meditative music as background for the tai chi.

Every day, there was church in the park. Groups gathered together to celebrate Nature, each other, and their own personal values.

What a wonderful way to reflect the deep, spiritual wonder of life. They may be godless, but they certainly have spirit, even the guy who stole my glasses.

Beggar on the street

I try to be kind, giving, and generous. I tithe and contribute to what I deem good causes. In China, as here at home, there were street beggars, and I would often give them money. My contributions were generous, paper stuff, not coins. The pedestrians, ever aware of what the foreigner did, not only noticed that I gave, but also how much.

I gave because I am thankful for all I have received and figured, that there, but by the grace of God, go I. I had so much and they had so little.

Well, the public reaction from the people on the street was almost explosive. An English-speaking person would invariably warn me not to give to these people. I was told they were part of a gang, with much money in their own right and were just acting as beggars, which happened regularly on the streets of Beijing and Shanghai. They also scolded and chastised me for giving so much. Someone called PPI about my giving and even the rather large amount (in their perspective) and one of the staff told Lovy about this terrible thing I was doing. Snitches!

One day, I turned a corner and lying on the street was a young, male beggar. I was shocked! His legs had been mangled at birth and he couldn't stand. He dragged himself along the sidewalk. The crowd swirled around him, almost stepping on him. He and I made eye contact and I was smitten with compassion.

His name was Bao Hai and I used to slip him a 100 RMB note ($12 US).

Through Agatha, my English-speaking assistant, I learned that he came from Shandong Province, one of the poorest provinces. He had been a good student, but his parents told him that schooling would be wasted and he should go to Shanghai to beg and send money home. Because their first-born was crippled, the government allowed his parents, poor peasant farmers, to have another child, making an exception to the one-child rule. Boa Hai has a normal, able-bodied brother.

I gave him a Chinese edition of Think and Grow Rich by Napoleon Hill. He began writing me letters in Chinese and Agatha translated them. We could communicate more deeply than through translated conversations with him lying on the sidewalk.

He invited Lovy and me to visit him and his parents in Shandong Province. One weekend Agatha, Lovy and I took a train-and-bus adventure into the real China countryside. We slept in a four-bed compartment as the train whistled into the night. First train, then bus, and, as the road got narrower and narrower, a cart.

A feast was prepared for us, and the villagers dropped by to take a look at the "rich" foreigners. Bao Hai had certainly been sending his money home, and his parents were living in an opulent style compared to the other villagers. My donations had helped buy a large TV, and a new, spacious home. What it did not cover was any plumbing improvements. When Nature called me, I had to go out back and squat on a typical Chinese squatter toilet over a cesspool of stinking, fly-infested human waste. I didn't know which way to face and was concerned that while balancing on my haunches, I might tip over.

I faced outward, and leaned over for safety, banging my head on a brick wall. When I returned, everyone looked frightened and asked how I was. I said fine, not realizing that my forehead was covered with red cement crumbs from its encounter with the brick wall.

Lovy put an immediate stop to my contributing to the furnishing of the family home in Shandong. She talked about contributing to our grandchildren's education fund.

After reading the book and my letters, Boa Hai returned home and started farming chickens and rabbits. He came to realize, as the book stated, "Whatever the mind of man can conceive and believe, he can achieve." I told Boa Hai that regardless of what his parents thought, he did not have to think of himself as a beggar. So he made, first in his mind, then with his body, the journey from begging on the streets of Shanghai to a being a chicken-and-rabbit farmer entrepreneur in Shandong.

CHAPTER SIX
- Shanghai Traffic
- Chinese Medicine

Shanghai Traffic

I recalled two phenomena from living in Richmond, B.C., for twenty-seven years.

- The influx of Orientals from Hong Kong, Taiwan and Mainland China changed the population mix among Caucasian, East Indian and Chinese.

- The Chinese drivers soon overtook women drivers as the ones to beware of on the roads. Their unpredictability, ignorance of common courtesies of the road, their seeming inattention to driving between the lines and at normal speeds, etc.

I took these prejudices with me to Shanghai. Traffic was horrific! Cars, taxis, buses, trucks, vans, motor-scooters, bicycles all drove at break-neck speeds really close to each other. There are no traffic-lane lines and traffic lights are ignored.

Lovy, with her new lease on life and zest for excitement and adventure, would stride confidently, purposefully, and safely through the maze.

I hesitated, trying to gauge my chances of survival, looking for the right moment to cross. In China, the right time is always "now." The Chinese can tell how long foreigners have been in

Shanghai by how long it takes us to cross the street. The quicker you cross, the longer you have been in China.

Newbies dither, swivel their heads anxiously trying to pace the flow, make false starts and repeatedly dart back to the safety of the sidewalk. Veterans move across confidently knowing they are safe in the midst of all the noise, horns, and vehicular mayhem. They meld with the flow.

People in the West jump off cliffs tied to a kite, kayak turbulent, white waters and jump out of airplanes for thrills. I could never do that.

But every time I crossed a street in Shanghai I got the same shot of adrenalin a skydiver gets. It provided me with my thrills for the day.

One day, while leaning on the balcony rail of our apartment and watching the passing scene, I became aware of the traffic pattern. It was full-bore traffic, and yet there was a pattern in the chaos: without lanes, lights or stop and go order, everything flowed. Cars, taxis, trucks, vans, buses, carts, scooter, people were all flowing. I didn't see many accidents, which was unbelievable to my Western eyes. The few I saw usually involved bicycles and buses. There were accidents and traffic deaths reported, although I never saw any. For a city of twenty million people there had to be, but I would say that the incidence was a much smaller ratio than in a North American city.

My paradigm shifted again: from the Chinese being the worst drivers in the world to being the best drivers, subject to driving in their own city and country. Again, this was another example of going with the flow.

Whenever there was an accident, no matter how minor,

immediately a crowd gathered and everyone had something to say. Even if they had not actually witnessed the event, they had an opinion just from viewing the situation. The policeman would make his decision based on the group discussion. This is consensus making of the Confucian way.

Here's another personal vignette about getting my Shanghai driver's license. I was impressed with the full battery of tests I had to take, which involved written and many machine/computer tests for spatial acuity, depth perception, etc. I had difficulty with language comprehension and reaction slowness. The middle-aged female monitors were most helpful and made sure this gweilo passed. I knew I really hadn't, but here is where saving face, even for a foreigner, paid off. Hey, I am a nice "round eyes" and they sensed I had crossed the bridge from judgment to trust and respect of all things Chinese.

I also received the license, without a driving test, Thank God, albeit, in a godless country!

Chinese Medicine

The left-brain, right-brain dichotomy showed up again in the field of medicine. The Western, left-brain approach is to go until we get sick. We see our doctor. Quick, Doc, fix me up, I gotta go! I'm busy! He prescribes a chemical pharmaceutical or takes a knife to our body.

The Chinese approach is a preventative, natural, long-term approach. They take herbs (natural plants), practice tai chi, yoga, attend daily church in the park, have acupuncture treatments to prevent sickness and they drink gallons of green tea.

They smile when they say we in the West pay the doctor

when we get sick. There, they stop paying the doctor when they get sick.

And they do get sick. In the hustle-bustle 24/7 beat of life, getting run down, burnt out is quite common. I know that getting sick is usually God's way of telling us to slow down, to take a rest. When I first arrived, I scoffed at and criticized a common practice. When a person got run down, they went to the hospital (doctors don't have offices, they all work in hospitals) and received some mysterious sort of intravenous injection for three to four hours, for one or two days, depending. When I asked what the injection was, no one seemed to know or care. It just worked.

I also got caught up in the race and from time to time got burnt out and stressed out. After I was open to things Chinese, I, too, went to the hospital for my injections. An extensive battery of tests was taken and the blood analyzed. Elements of what my blood showed I was low in were concocted, plus appropriate antibiotics into an injectible mixture tailor-made cocktail for my condition. Within six to eight hours, my blood was replenished and I was on the go again.

Most ex-pats don't trust Chinese hospitals and go to foreign clinics with Western-trained medical people. They charge exorbitant rates, because nearly all the patients have corporate benefit packages. The leading, Chinese teaching hospitals have outpatient departments specifically staffed for foreigners. The fee is ten times or more what the Chinese native pays, but a fraction of what you would be charged at a Western medical clinic. Once I learned the system, I got my acupuncture doctor or Michelle, my Chinese wife, to register me under my Chinese name, Tianen, and I would be charged native rates. Several times she called on a school classmate who was a physician and I received red-carpet treatment, moving quickly to the head of a long line. While seeing a doctor in a Chinese hospital registered as a Chinese (nobody noticed or cared that my eyes were the wrong shape) they would search the hospital and hustle up a student nurse who spoke English.

I found the Chinese doctors competent and open to suggestions. The Confucian philosophy is about consensus, not one-man rule. They usually worked with a younger doctor or medical student and were polite and attentive in receiving, and acting on the others' ideas.

When I was diagnosed with a prostate cancer, which metastasized to my lungs, I began a massive comprehensive program that covered all fronts: West, East, and spiritual.

- Western medicine, hormone injection
- Reduced my consumption of red meat
- Ate more fresh vegetables
- Began yoga
- Began acupuncture treatments for energy balancing
- Started drinking green tea
- Started drinking soya milk daily
- Began ingesting traditional Chinese herbs
- Had a special Chinese tea for prostate cancer mixed
- Affirmed, visualized and believed in a miracle healing
- Prayed

The Prostate Specific Antigen test (PSA) is the most commonly used screening tool for detecting prostate cancer. When I was diagnosed, my PSA reading was 28.6. My prostate biopsy slides had cancer cells on ten of the eleven slides and my right lung was covered with cancer nodules.

After the first three months, when my PSA reading dropped from 28.6 to 0.016 and all the cancer nodules on my lung had vanished, the Canadian specialists could not believe my results. They even questioned the diagnosis and didn't see the humor in my scientific assessment that "Doc, maybe this is a miracle." I dared not add that an element of Traditional Chinese Medicine (TCM) could also have contributed to my cure. They failed to see any humor in such unscientific, frivolous comments.

Today, five years later, with complete testing every three months, I remain free of cancer.

It wasn't as easy as it sounds. My first prostate specialist, who had put me on hormone injection therapy with amazing results, wanted to keep injecting me every three months. This was a female hormone designed to reduce my testosterone levels. Every three months, he and I would argue about continuing the injections. I didn't want to take a female hormone that affected my flab content, my breasts and my libido. He stressed that I was lucky the cancer was in remission. I called it a miracle and I was cured.

Finally, he referred me to Dr. Goldenberg who practiced alternative hormone therapy. If my PSA was below 4, no injection. However, if it was above 4, I had to take it until it came down. I have not had to take any more injections.

CHAPTER SEVEN
Dining in China

Food is important in all cultures, but in China, it plays a paramount role as the tool for face and guanxi.

Business eating is where guanxi is established. To get to know another person and to build trust, eating together is necessary. The Chinese don't eat at their desks, and they don't rush out to the nearest fast-food joint. It is a specific time for talking and getting to know the other person. Typically, business is not discussed. That's done during the many business meetings.

The business banquet is the pinnacle of guanxi building, celebrating, and or honoring guests.

We would gather at one of thousands (in a city of 20 million) of huge, ornately designed Chinese restaurants, usually on the second floor. Courteous, friendly, happy staff, with wireless buds in their ears, directed you to your table or private room while waiters and waitresses rushed around with plates of sumptuous, gorgeous-looking and luscious-smelling food.

A Chinese banquet is not only a culinary feast and experience; it is a visual and auditory experience. It starts with seven to eight cold appetizers of the most intriguing items. That's followed by twelve to fifteen hot courses: beef, pork, chicken, duck, two fish (selected from the water tanks at the entrance, inspected and approved at table side), and all sorts of vegetables (no cold salads as we know them). I love salad and made my own at home. My Chinese father-in-law used to laugh and call me, in Chinese, a grass eater. The huge lazy-Susan platform keeps rotating, and you pick up these juicy, tasty morsels with your chopsticks as they go by. Usually two kinds of soups and rice are served near the end of the meal. When they serve the watermelon, you know the meal is over. There is no happy hour, no cocktail before dinner, mostly orange juice though and no lingering over a cigar and liqueur. After the watermelon, you get up and go.

I attended many banquets, but one, as the guest of the chairman of Jia Ling Motorcycles, was more memorable than the rest. Jia Ling produced more than one million motorcycles a year plus over one and a half million motorcycle engines for other manufacturers. DMG was staging a large international exhibition for Jai Ling in Chongqing in Sichuan Province. We planned it as a Las Vegas style event: strobe lights, large overhead movie screens, blasting music, and many gorgeous, leggy ladies.

We were mobbed. The mayor, who heard of our sound and light show, couldn't get near our area. The press of the people damaged the stands and the grounds and caused us problems with the building management. We ran out of literature. For a guy from North Battleford, Saskatchewan, Canada, it was an amazing spectacle to be at the center of.

On the last evening, the Jia Ling chairman staged a banquet for DMG's senior people. Protocol stipulates that the most senior person from each company sit together at the head of the round table with the rest sitting in descending order. As group general manager, I sat next to the chairman. Business dining is a ritualistic affair based on guanxi and face.

A row of drinking glasses was placed in front of me — for water, beer, wine, and maotai. Maotai is made from wheat and sorghum and has an alcohol content of 55 per cent. It is a clear, white liquid and you drink it from small, shot-type glasses. Clearly from some foreigners, like me a lethal drink. Chairman Mao served maotai at state dinners during Richard Nixon's state visit to China. I'd had maotai before and it was awful, had a nasty aftertaste and didn't agree with my body. The waiter filled the chairman's glass and then mine. I was crushed with cultural and male, macho pressure.

I wanted to match my honored host, not lose face with my Chinese managers and be one of the boys. So when the chairman toasted us and downed his maotai, we all drank. As soon as the stuff hit my system, I knew that if it continued, and it does, my concern would not be about losing face, but losing it all. I had a choice: drink another maotai and get sick there or rush to the washroom, or put my hand over the glass as the waiter started to fill it. I could hold my own with the beer and red wine, but I couldn't handle the maotai.

I put my hand over the empty glass.

The second, the very second, the chairman observed my action, he ordered everyone's maotai glasses removed from the table. This was his way of showing me respect and saving my face. If I didn't drink maotai, no one would. In actual fact, I felt I had lost face because my behavior had affected the drinking enjoyment of everyone else. They loved maotais and company banquets were some of the few times they could enjoy them. But that was a Western reaction. The Chinese are non-judgmental and acritical. So we never skipped a beat, drank red wine and beer and continued with the party. No fuss, no embarrassment, just Confucian face saving.

In the excellent book, Nixon in China: The Week That

Changed the World, Margaret MacMillian detailed the former
U.S. president's encounter with maotais. Future secretary of
State, Alexander Haig, having witnessed Nixon's slight tolerance
for alcohol and having experienced the potent Chinese maotai
himself, warned in a top-secret cable,

"UNDER NO, REPEAT, NO CIRCUMSTANCES SHOULD
THE PRESIDENT ACTUALLY DRINK FROM HIS GLASS IN
RESPONSE TO BANQUET TOASTS."

The common greeting in China is "Have you eaten yet?" When
I first arrived, I was perplexed by this question and hesitated
before answering because I didn't know if they were inviting me
to eat with them. I was still uncomfortable about eating with a
Chinese person that I didn't know well.

Here, on this side of the water, when you meet someone you
ask, "How are you?" It's a greeting. You don't want to know about
their lower back pain or whether their boss is a pain farther down.
You're supposed to reply, "I'm fine, thank you."

In China, "Have you eaten yet?" is also just a greeting. You're
supposed to answer, "Yes, I have eaten." If you have eaten, you
are fine.

In China, with its turbulent past and a billion plus, there
were times when many people did go hungry. Millions died of
starvation during Mao's Cultural Revolution. So, "Have you eaten
yet?" does have its roots in the significance of real food shortages
and not being able to eat.

Ordinary family meals, with four to five cold appetizer dishes
followed by eight to ten courses, are eaten around a round table.
Those meals, with everyone taking food from communal plates,
are always a happy time. This certainly creates a warm, family

celebration atmosphere for every meal, not just for special occasions. The noises, the smells, the sights, the constant chatter, are happy family times.

In the West, the largest portion of household expenses goes to the upkeep of spacious houses. In China, the largest expenditure is food, eating and going out for breakfast, brunch, lunch and dinners, with family, relatives and friends. The seeds of guanxi are planted and nurtured at these meals.

The Chinese are opened-minded about eating all sorts of things that we would gag on. In Southern China, in the Guangzhou area markets, you can buy dog and cat meat for dinner.

During a business luncheon one day, the waiter brought a burlap bag to the table and our host looked into it and nodded. I had seen the waiter bring us live fish from the tanks for approval, so I wondered why they put the fish in a burlap bag. It wasn't a fish, it was a live snake. I ate snake for lunch that day. I've eaten roasted cockroaches and duck tongues.

I could handle these, but not maotai? Here is how I managed it. I told myself, "Ern, it's all in your mind. Your body recognizes this only as protein. To your digestive system, it isn't snake or cockroach. It's just protein. It's your mind that messes it up." Maotai was not mental, it was physical. My body rejected it, but not protein.

Don't let these little side experiences taint your impression of Chinese food and cooking. It's wonderful. The myriad ways they prepare all the dishes is fantastic: the tastes, the colors, and the presentation. Eating in China is a wonderful experience.

The amazing thing is that you never see fat Chinese people. On the city streets you are beginning to see more and more fat Chinese children as McDonald's, KFC, and other fast-food restaurants, make their presence felt in every city.

The Chinese drink copious amounts of green tea, which constantly flushes fats from their system. An ingredient in green tea joins with fat, makes it water soluble, and so it goes.

CHAPTER EIGHT

- Living in a Chinese Family
- Accidents Happen
- Chinese Education
- Sex in Shanghai

Living in a Chinese Family

It was one thing to work with Chinese people, have Chinese friends and Chinese clients, but one of my most enriching experiences was living as a member of a middle-class Chinese family.

For two years, I was married to a wonderful, beautiful and successful Shanghainese businesswoman, Michelle, who had a seven-year-old daughter.

All I had heard about and read about the Chinese culture, I was able to experience from the inside. Family, friends and health awareness are integral parts of their culture.

There are no nursing homes in China. Confucian philosophy dictates the relationship between the son and his parents. It is expected that the son will look after his parents in their old age. A room is set aside for the eventual occupation of his remaining parent in the son's home. Because of the one-child policy, sons are preferred. The current birth ratio in China is about 90 girls for every 100 boys. Various methods are used to tilt the scale. Abortions are common, and encouraged, as a form of birth control. Birth selection comes about from ultrasound scans, which can determine the sex of the unborn child. The 90/100 ratio is going to catch up eventually. It is a fact of life that young men, with testosterone coursing through their systems, need young women somewhere along the line. Already we hear of young women being kidnapped from Viet Nam, Thailand and Cambodia and brought into the hinterland to satisfy nature's demands.

The other fact I observed is the only child syndrome on a national scale. You know, that the only child has certain benefits, advantages and personality characteristics that children with siblings don't have. Right now, in China there are more only child kids (over three hundred and fifty million) than the entire population of the U.S. These children have two sets of grandparents, aunts and uncles doting over them, doing everything for them, including thinking for them. They are all little emperors and empresses. Imagine as they mature and take their place in society, what traits and expectations they will bring to the political and corporate world of China?

We talked about friendship and guanxi and how school classmates maintain their connection throughout the years of career growth.

Deep friendship is very important and not limited to social or job networking. Suppose a classmate is experiencing marriage difficulties. It is quite normal that a group of classmates, male and female, would band together and if needed, travel large distances to spend time with the troubled couple. The men would meet with the husband; the women would meet with the wife. Then, the women and men would meet and discuss the situation. Then a combined dinner would take place, with more meetings later. The purpose is not for intrusion or fixing, but each person and their happiness is important, also for face. So, no effort is too much to bring peace to the couple. I was so impressed with this kind of activity, and again it reminded me that the Chinese are really a peace-saving and peace-making culture if for no other reason than to save face. Everybody's face.

Health is an important issue in a Chinese family. My father-in-law and mother-in-law were in their mid-seventies and they were in much better physical condition than I was. My father-in-law for the past forty years, daily went to the park and did tai chi for forty minutes and he walked for at least forty minutes. One day, when it was very cold and blustery, he did his ritual on the balcony of our apartment. I watched him from the comfort and warmth of the inside. It was fascinating. He spent about a quarter of the time slapping and massaging his face. My wife slapped her face while she was doing her morning toilette. That might explain why Chinese people have smooth, wrinkle free faces, no matter what their age. My mother-in-law, just standing in the kitchen, was constantly making tai chi moves as she walked and talked

Accidents happen

One morning, while walking down the street with Michelle, I slammed into a metal sheet protruding from the walkway. I stumbled as blood gushed from my forehead. Immediately, a crowd gathered, police were called and the discussion began. Towels and water appeared. With much discussion, my fate was sealed and a policeman drove me to the hospital on his motorcycle.

I received seven or eight stitches and then hopped on the back of the motorcycle and was taken to the police station to file a report.

I was having a fantastic experience, racing through the busy streets of Shanghai on a police bike. As we passed my wife walking to the station, I waved, like a kid on a circus ride. The look on her face was far from joyful. She had lost face being with a gweilo who walked into objects on the street, and we were going to the police station to file a report and negotiate payment for our hospital bill.

At the station, the theatre began. After initial indifference from the office police, Michelle (after I've been briefed and assumed a painful, angry and serious countenance) talked loudly on her cell, actually to her sister, but making it sound like she was talking to the Canadian consulate about this terrible thing that has happened to a Canadian on the streets of Shanghai. That got the cops' attention. Three representatives of varying levels of hierarchy from the construction company appeared quickly. The police interviewed us separately. Back and forth, matching, pairing statements. With room-to-room shuttle diplomacy, without lawyers, we received cash on the spot for our hospital expenses. Actually, we could have received whatever we asked for. The construction company had much to lose from the Shanghai city government for sloppy, shoddy sidewalk protection.

Chinese Education
During the high immigration of Hong Kong Chinese into Richmond, precipitated by fear of what would happen when Communist China took Hong Kong back, our children were students in the public school system. The new Chinese students quickly took all the top scholastic spots, winning all the awards, bursaries and scholarships. Naturally, there was a certain amount of resentment from the local students and parents about this "oriental invasion."

There is a simple explanation for their superior classroom performance: their study habits.

Chinese parents are obsessed with their children excelling in school to ensure a future of riches. The driving force is tied in with the Chinese cultural tradition that children look after the parents in their later years. Children with the best marks are the best insurance, even better than London Life's Freedom 55 plan.

In the West, you choose and apply to the school you want to attend and then based on your marks, you are accepted, or not. In China, you have no choices. The Chinese national educational system is based entirely on merit. Your marks determine which school you qualify to get into. In 2006, 9.5 million high-school graduates sat down for three days of tests to determine which 2.6 million would enter Chinese universities in September.

Just before returning to Canada, I taught English for a semester in a first-tier Shanghai high school. Each high school had a native English-speaking teacher to counter the Chinglish phenomenon.

At first, I was troubled because the students kept falling asleep in my class. Then, I realized they were dead tired. Teachers gave them loads of assignments and harangued them if they didn't complete them. Their parents woke them early to study and kept them up late studying for the college entrance exams, their one and only chance to get into university. Their future was determined by these entrance exams. They had to forgo all TV, sports, socializing. Study. Study. Study.

In a rush of empathy and a desire to help, I gave them research data from the Harvard Medical School Psychology Department that proved what they studied when they were tired, they would not remember at the exam. To improve their marks, they needed to get a good night's sleep.

I gave them reprints of the findings and told them that if they chose to tell their parents, the parents would not buy it.

One parent, when his son showed him my documentation, said, "Don't listen to that crazy foreigner. You study. You will sleep when you are old!"

I enjoyed and admired these students. They were interested in the West. They respected the West and the U.S. and its accomplishments. They envied the Western educational system that provided freedom of study. While they recognized they were better students and would get higher marks than a Western student, they also gave credit for the innovation and creativity that a free system encourages. They would repeatedly say, apologetically, "A Chinese person has never received a Nobel Peace Prize."

I also attribute much of this to the only child syndrome.

They are not encouraged to have initiative and independence. Everything is done for them, except study, study, and study.

Sex in Shanghai
The global economy is based on sex.

A baby is often the result when two people have sexual intercourse. This begins a spending spree that includes increasing purchases of food, clothing, housing, furniture, appliances, transportation, schools, hospitals, government buildings, etc, etc. This is the simple basis of economic growth. People spending money. Factor in that close to seven billion people, many having sex this very minute, leading to more births. You do the math.

All this spending requires manufacturing plants for the goods and providing of services. Companies, industries and countries are started and run by Type A personalities with above average testosterone levels, which provide the push to make things happen. Napoleon Hill in Think and Grow Rich addressed this issue as sexual transmutation. This explains why many powerful business leaders and powerful politicians are called charismatic and appear to be highly sexed. Some feed this drive within the confines of marriage and committed relationships; many do not. This is always chronicled in the papers and on CNN.

I began this discussion on sex from a global economic perspective because sex is not a moral, ethical issue; it is a biological fact.

So, what about sex in China, sex in Shanghai? My comments are limited to my personal observations and what others with more direct knowledge and experience have shared with me.

First, there is above the line and below the line. Above the line, other than for the young, beautiful Chinese ladies wearing long, red dresses with slits dangerously high on the thigh at most official events, sex is visibility absent.

Of course, it's an intimate, personal matter in all cultures. In China, with their indirectness of communication, their shyness, and face saving, it's hidden. The government is vigilant about pornography, although porn CDs are readily available on the back streets from young, impoverished mothers from the countryside. They are obviously victims and agents of organized porn groups.

Now, let's go below the line. I will examine three areas of sex in the city.

- Sex for foreigners

- Sex for Chinese men of wealth and the growing middle class

- Sex for the common Chinese man.

The male foreigner arriving in Shanghai will be awestruck by the number of striking women dressed in modern, attractive, and provocative attire. Shanghainese women are known for their beauty and sharpness. These ladies hold the West, Westerners and the Western lifestyle as the epitome of how they want to live. The perfect scenario is to latch onto an older foreigner, supposedly wealthy with access to the U.S. and U.S. citizenship for education of her children. Upon the elder partner's earthly departure, she stays or returns home to her family with sufficient means to provide for her parents in an envied style of comfort. So the age-old, trans-cultural Venus flytrap of sex arises with easy and frequent availability.

Simply put, there is much good, clean sex available to foreigners.

I am not referring to the sex trade, which is also, omnipresent and omni-available.

China is not burdened with the sin and guilt associated with sex in our society. It's a natural, clean, enjoyable activity. It was interesting to observe how many men in public washrooms wash their hands before approaching the urinal. I guess they figured their hands were dirty from handling money, doors, etc. and their organ was clean from the morning shower and clean shorts, so they washed their hands first.

The Western washes his hands after. We carry from our early upbringing that that part of our body is dirty, whether it was just washed and packed away in clean underwear or not.

For the increasing number of wealthy Chinese men, it has been traditionally, and still is, accepted to have mistresses and to provide them with downtown apartments and all the accoutrements of success. This is usually not blatant, so as to save face for his wife and family.

I was entertained one evening by a Chinese businessman who wanted some favors from my company. He was accompanied by his gorgeous girlfriend. After a late dinner, they took me to a karaoke bar and I knew that a foursome could easily and quickly be arranged.

On another occasion, when we were making a corporate presentation to a possible client and his company contingent, he also had his lady friend, who he introduced as his wife. He had to do a fast shuffle when an aide whispered that his real wife had just entered the building.

Love, marriage, family is complicated in any culture. I got the feeling that with the super level of confidence and high expectations of the wives, frequent withholding of sexual accessibility was a bargaining chip that often drove the man to seek outsourcing services. It's much the same in most countries. The male vs. female game has been thus played since ancient times everywhere.

For the common man, away from the hot throb of the city scene of classy bars and lounges, every street with stores on it has a plethora of beauty parlors, which also have an inventory of beauties who are more than willing to go to the second floor of the establishment.

Early in my Chinese marriage, Michelle went with me to the local beauty parlor to arrange a haircut for me. She came to give instructions in Chinese to the beauticians and was quite clear that this gweilo was to get his hair trimmed only, without a trip upstairs.

There are many massage parlors, which vary considerably in price, ambience, quality of the masseuse or masseur, and comprehensiveness of services offered. The usual menu includes foot massage, body massage and oil massage. Additions may include a variety of Chinese medicinal services; include cupping — heated vessels placed on the back. The high-end versions of massage parlors are called spas. The highest end tends to cater exclusively to wealthy women; they offer a variety of beauty treatments, including skin whitening.

A notch down are spas that cater to both men and women, offering single or dual massage tables for treatments by one or two massage therapists for one or two customers. A hot tub and sauna may be provided in the higher-end establishments, along with soothing music.

The more reputable establishments don't offer sexual favors, but many parlors do. Some might offer an excellent massage by a trained masseuse with good experience, with or without intimate contact while others might offer a decent massage for a low price, with the possibility of negotiation for additional services. The range of skill and experience is as great from spa to parlor, as it is within a given establishment. You throw the dice and take your chances, but a great massage can be obtained at varying price levels, regardless of the ambience or location.

Part II:

The Lessons

LESSON ONE
Open your mind, change your paradigm

Ignorance, Arrogance, Judgment = A Wall.

My mandate at PPI was to develop a self-empowered Chinese management team and staff to run the day-to-day operations while Dan was in Hollywood directing and producing two feature-length movies.

PPI had 60 Chinese managers, supervisors and staff in the Beijing and Shanghai production studios.

I was coming from Canada,	I was going to China
a developed country	a developing country
a democratic country	a dictatorship
a Christian (?) country	a godless country
a capitalistic economy	a communistic economy

Naturally, I judged their culture and business sense, seeing it through the filters of what I had been conditioned to believe: that our way was the right way, the only way, the truth and the light.

I was ignorant of their 5,000 year history, culture and tradition. I viewed them as backward, their ways inferior.

I had a mental swagger perpetuated by my belief that the West was superior and more advanced. I believed we were right and they were wrong.

I had built a wall in my mind that separated instead of bridging two people, two companies, two cultures and two countries.

This didn't cause fisticuffs in the boardrooms. No, no. We are too civilized and the Chinese are too polite to tell it like it is. However, more than 90 per cent of communication is non-verbal, and that part neither side can hide. I was behaving and believing like a true gweilo.

What happened?

Nothing!

Just smiles, gifts, dinners, meetings.

Nothing happened.

Zero.

No progress.

The hot shot, know-it-all, we-are-the- good-guys, let-me-show-you-how-we-do-things-in-the-West consultant was not getting the job done, was not getting anything done.

My two-year contract had a three-month probationary clause.

Dan told me he would be watching to see how the staff accepted the "foreigner," which was a direct reflection on how effective I would be in completing the assignment.

Nothing was happening. How could it, with my wall up?

The wall was my mind, my perception of the Chinese and all things Chinese.

I was running out of time. The pressure was on.

The Fool had to produce. Dan's Osho Zen Tarot cards weren't going to help me here.

Results were needed.

My China adventure was in jeopardy.

My wife was with me. What would our children back in Canada think?

Dad returning home an international failure.

Woe is me.

What could I do?

Forty per cent of top foreign executives and managers don't complete their contracts, returning home with their families; broken men, burnt out, often with the family in tatters. I worked as a volunteer at a Shanghai crisis line for ex-pats and heard first hand the difficulties some families experienced dealing with the culture shock of integrating into this new world. These were successful people with many other successful foreign postings: Japan, Singapore, Australia, etc.

But this was China and I was on my way to joining that forty per cent.

The global consulting firm, PricewaterhouseCoopers, with its worldwide constituency and a large client base in China, had conducted a study of internal burnout at high executive levels and arrived at the forty per cent number.

A more recent and more comprehensive study conducted by the global search firm Korn/Ferry International found that while China is among the most attractive places for executives to take an international assignment, it's also the most difficult place to succeed. Most leave before the end of their stint. The most common reason for failure was not fitting into the local culture. Other reasons were family or personal and not getting enough direction and support from head office.

This was a delicate topic that wasn't discussed in polite company. We are talking about the mental and emotional states of men leading large organizations under extreme pressure. They were dealing with Chinese cultural issues, with management and general staff, a wife and family caught in a strange land, strange language, and strange culture. They traveled a lot, had crushing workloads and the endless, tedious meetings with clients, government and suppliers made it worse. Bosses back home were unsympathetic and only questioned costs, time delays, lack of profits and market share. That's the life of corporate leaders, but it's magnified in the stressful, cross-cultural, high profile China situation.

The personality profile of these individuals usually is of a strong willed, dominating person with a drive to achieve. They aren't right-brained individuals prone to introspection or overly concerned with feelings. Personal and corporate image, and pride keep these matters hidden. One of the few places the problems was aired was at the Long Bar, at the Shanghai Center, where all the hard-drinking executives sought solace with beautiful Shanghainese women offering respite from their hectic schedules.

The men would never phone a crisis line. The macho, male ego doesn't need that. These guys don't think they need anything. Many HR directors are frustrated that their key executives think their staff needs training, but they don't. And if they don't need training, they certainly don't need cross-cultural coaching. Hard-driving bosses don't do soft, fuzzy stuff.

As a volunteer on the Shanghai Ex-pat Crisis line, I took many calls from the wives adrift in an unknown society, their man always at work, on a trip or too tired when he came home. The wives worried about the lovely, smart, female executive assistants their husbands spent so much time with, including traveling. The wives worried about their children with all the normal stages of puberty and adolescence, except in a strange country, thousands of miles from home, family, friends and support group.

Alcohol, drugs, sex were the same as back home, only magnified because of the isolation in the middle of millions of strange people they didn't understand.

That was what the danger pay with the comprehensive, ex-pat packages were for. I wasn't in their league, but I was dealing with my own cross-cultural stress.

My moment of truth came when Lovy pointed her finger in my face and gave me my wake-up call. (referred to in Chapter Four: Lovy) I realized I had to change because going home was not an option.

When I got the finger pointing, the cursing, and the frustration out of the way, I took a look in the mental mirror. The focal point for all businesses and business people is results. A glimmer appeared in the form of my question about results.

If these people were so backward, so behind the times, how come their economy had been growing nine to twelve per cent consistently for twenty-eight years?

Not one democratic capitalistic economy has shown that growth rate consistently for the past twenty-eight years. We get excited about two to three percent growth and that's sporadic.

Hmmmm? How come?

So began my business and cultural odyssey into how and why the Chinese system gets results. It is all about results. With my Western mind creaking open, I was exposed to the delightful history, culture, traditions and values of one of the world's oldest, most fascinating cultures, the most populous country, the world's biggest market, the world's largest manufacturing center.

I changed my mind about China.

I changed my paradigm about life and peace.

I began to understand the people.

I accepted them.

I adapted to their philosophy.

I adopted their values.

I fell in love with China, its story and its people.

I changed.

And, I started getting results.

My two-year contract turned lasted five and one half years.

The walls of ignorance, arrogance and judgment came crashing down and were replaced with new learning, respect and understanding for others different from me.

When I returned home, I again had to make it back across the bridge to re-enter and accept once again the culture and society that I had grown up in, but had been absent from for seven years. This is a common challenge for returning ex-pats.

Life is about bridges.

Success in the global market is about bridges.

Peace in the world is about bridges.

It is about bridges, not walls!

LESSON TWO

Communists get things done, too

1.3 and 5,000.

The population of the U.S. is 300 million.

China's population is 1.3 billion.

Stop for a moment and consider the respective jobs and responsibilities of U.S. President George W. Bush and Chinese President Hu Jintao.

The principles of governance may be similar, but the numbers are staggering.

The burden of governing 1.3 billion people compared to 300 million is lost on most Westerners who are quick to criticize how Chinese leaders govern, yes, control the masses, while nurturing the hottest and largest economy in the history of the world.

People often ask me about corruption in China.

I reply with a question, "Do you have corruption in America?

China has everything that the U.S. does, only in larger amounts.

You do the math. On the ratio of corruption in our democratic, political system of 300 million people and then that of China with 1.3 billion. China has 4.3 times the people, so logically you could expect 4.3 times as much corruption.

Some Chinese friends pointed out that democracy is an adversarial system that prevents an elected politician from working directly for the best interests of his constituents and the country. When politicians are elected democratically, it seems that their priorities fall this way:

1. To keep their job and get re-elected.

2. To prove that the opposing party is 100 per cent always wrong, incompetent, sleazy, and untrustworthy.

3. To satisfy special interest groups and lobbyists that finance the party to keep it in power.

4. Finally, then, they consider what might be good for the country

It is exciting to watch how the U.S. is approaching the rising profile of China. Traditionally, the bi-partisan split is left wing vs. right wing. The left wing, Democratic, liberal, right brain spectrum would be more supportive to China. The right wing, Republican, conservative, left brain would be hesitant, yea, resistant accommodating the Red Threat. That is exactly how it is currently being played out. This might, however, be changing.

Enter a new player on the Republican team.

Henry Paulson, as U.S. Treasury Secretary and the former chairman of Goldman Sachs, has excellent guanxi with the highest levels of the Chinese government. He made over 70 trips to China as CEO of Goldman Sachs, has paid his dues and earned their trust and respect. When Congress was about to introduce a 27 per cent import tariff on Chinese imports, that vote was delayed. Mr. Paulson has worked hard convincing his Republican buddies on how to do good business with the Chinese.

In China, under Confucian influence of respect for hierarchy, consensus, face, and guanxi, a benevolent dictatorship seems to be working. They do have major problems, as every government does:

- a restless, impoverished farming population

- pollution

- a banking and legal system that needs fixing

- a full throttle economy that needs cooling off and controlling

China does have its skeletons:

- Tibet

- Tiananmen Square

- Falun Gong

- the Cultural Revolution

- human rights practices

Of course, they also have personality differences, varying levels of personal ambitions and the polarity of progressive vs. conservative pressures, but not the open divisiveness of partisanship. Even though it is a one-party state, the government is sensitive to the internal murmurings and rumblings of the people, and there are many. They don't need another grass roots revolution, which is why they came down so hard on Falun Gong cult. The leadership is also sensitive to how the rest of the world sees China. Our markets and resources are important to them and it wants to showcase the New China at the 2008 Olympics in Beijing, the 2010 World Expo in Shanghai, WTO, etc.

China is rapidly becoming a world superpower. They're doing it peacefully by building relationships: forging, trusting, win-win, long-term, mutual benefit relationships with other nations.

The richness of their history, traditions, and values is a wonderful strengthening asset for them and helps them handle the amazing growth they're experiencing. They enjoy a quiet confidence that a people who have been around a long time and experienced everything — ups, downs, power, occupation by foreign powers, revolution. The pressures of sudden, dramatic change are also affecting every part of their culture: generational, governmental, family, business, educational, etc.

When your culture, your history and background are 5,000 years old you have a completely different perception of yourself, your family, your country, of time, of the rest of the world, than if you lived in a country that is 230 years old.

When I arrived in Shanghai, it seemed as if the whole city was under construction. It already had a massive freeway system that matched or surpassed the one in Los Angeles, and a skyline of space age, futuristic, skyscrapers like something from a Star Wars movie. These were preparing for Oct. 1, 1999, the New China's 50th anniversary.

In my view, there was no way they would all be completed by Oct. 1. But they were!

There are many reasons for China's stupendous economic growth. Certainly one of them is that they are a benevolent dictatorship.

When the government decides it wants to do something, it forges ahead, without the complexities of democracy. It doesn't have to worry about:

- the loyal opposition

- special interest groups

- lobbyists

- activists

- advocates

- protesters

- financial contributors

- unions

- layers of paper and policy.

They just do it!

THE THREE GORGES DAM PROJECT

The dam, seventeen years in the making, is one of the technological marvels of the world. Two thousand years ago, the Chinese built The Great Wall, which is visible from the moon.

The Three Gorges Dam is the modern equivalent of the Great Wall.

- It's the world's largest water conservation and flood-control project

- It's the world's largest hydro-power plant

- It allows ocean going ships to penetrate the heartland of China, opening up its vast resources and markets

- 2.5 million people are being resettled

- 1,599 industrial enterprises, including power, telecommunications, harbors, plants, roads are being relocated

- 250,000 workers have been employed on the project

The 2.5 million people being resettled, who were not living in the finest digs, will get a cash settlement, plus two options.

New cities are being built above the new water line and new, free homes will be given to those who stay. Those who don't want to stay can resettle in the larger cities such as Shanghai, Beijing and Guangzhou. The government will supply cash, transportation and new homes there. Older people are choosing to stay in the new cities and towns while younger people are opting for a new beginning in the larger cities.

LESSON THREE
Confucius says.....
China: godless, but not heathen!

Confucius, the most influential man in Chinese history, was born out of wedlock in 551 BC. His father had nine daughters and one crippled son. At age seventy, he mated with another woman, who was 15, hoping to get a healthy son. His father died when Confucius was three and his mother raised him in poverty.

He rose in the state government to the position of Justice Minister, but around age fifty, resigned and embarked on a twelve-year odyssey around China. When he returned home, he spent his last years teaching and writing. He died at seventy-two.

One of his deepest teachings and most difficult for Westerners to understand is the power of example instead of strict rules of behavior. Here we see again the interplay between the right brain and left-brain: high context vs. low context style of communication. This indirect way of his teaching still permeates China culture.

When his stables burnt down, Confucius said, "Was anyone hurt?" He did not ask about the horses. At that time, a horse was worth ten times as much as a stableman. By not asking about the horses, he demonstrated his priority, which was human beings. He made his points by indirectness, through casual reference, slight mention, and innuendo, even a slight nod.

He championed strong family loyalty, respect for elders and ancestor worship.

Among the important ethical concepts are:

1. Short-term pleasure is bad, while trying to do the proper things at the right time is better.

2. His moral system is based on kindness, empathy and understanding others, rather than divinely ordained rules. Virtue is based upon harmony with other people. This was the root of face and guanxi.

And so this man, who lived 500 years before Jesus, developed a code of behavior on how to treat others. This is not a religion. There are no god, no churches, no bible, no priests, and no dogma, just rational reasons how people and government should behave. Confucius remains the dominant Chinese philosopher, both morally and politically. His ideas are the official moral code and political doctrine of the state.

Politically, his ideas have been and are taught in all public services courses for civil servants, bureaucrats and potential leaders. The government supports and promotes Confucianism as an example for the conduct of government. It was his view that the way to change society is through education. He advocated happiness for the common people rather than pleasure for their rulers, reduction of taxes, mitigation of severe punishments and the avoidance of wars.

If you wish to do successful business in China, you had better have an understanding of the people and their cultural background.

Simply put, Confucianism is:

*   to love others

- to honor one's parents
- to honor elders
- to do what is right instead of what is advantageous
- to practice "reciprocity"
- to not do to others what you would not want done to you
- to rule by moral examples instead of by force and violence

The influence of these beliefs can be seen in every-day Chinese society. At work, there is a Confucian emphasis

- on interdependent relationships,
- on consensus, and
- on respect for hierarchy.

Once I became aware of this important part of the Chinese culture, I understood so much more clearly why they acted, behaved and did things the way they did. It was enlightening. Here are some of his authentic quotations:

Confucius say....

> To be able to practice five things everywhere under heaven constitutes perfect virtue ... gravity, generosity of soul, sincerity, earnestness, and kindness

> I hear, I know. I see, I remember. I do, I understand.

> Choose a job you love, and you will never have to work a day in your life

> Better a diamond with a flaw than a pebble without.

Real knowledge is to know the extent of one's ignorance.

Our greatest glory is not in never falling, but in rising every time we fall.

To know what is right and not to do it is the worst cowardice.

The strength of a nation derives from the integrity of the home.

It is better to light one small candle than to curse the darkness.

It is more shameful to distrust our friends than to be deceived by them.

There is an alternative philosophy in China called Taoism, based on the Tao Te Ching, written by Lao Tze. It precepts differ from the practical and rational Confucianism, which urges the individual to follow a logical and constructive path in society.

 Taoism urges believers to find The Way within themselves and through Nature. In Taoism we find the concept and yin/yang symbol. Taoism is about balance and forging harmony out of conflict and tension.

Tao (pronounced Dow) can be roughly translated as path, or *the way*. It is basically indefinable. It has to be experienced. It "refers to a power which envelops surrounds and flows through all things, living and non-living." The Tao regulates natural processes and nourishes balance in the Universe. It embodies the harmony of opposites (i.e. there would be no love without hate, no light without dark, no male without female).

http://www.religioustolerance.org/taoism.htm

Quotations:

- *"Be still like a mountain and flow like a great river."* Lao Tze

- *"We believe in the formless and eternal Tao, and we recognize all personified deities as being mere human constructs. We reject hatred, intolerance, and unnecessary violence, and embrace harmony, love and learning, as we are taught by Nature. We place our trust and our lives in the Tao that we may live in peace and balance with the Universe, both in this mortal life and beyond."*

LESSON FOUR

FACE
It is all about respect.

My parents loved my sister and me, and provided for our physical, educational, and religious needs. They did the best they could. In their desire for us to succeed, they criticized everything we did. They never gave positive recognition or approval no matter how well we did. I grew up in a critical and judgmental environment.

That same trend continued when I started working. Most managers played the cop role, correcting what we did wrong, and pounded us if we continued to get it wrong.

Newspapers, TV, magazines, radio all told us about what was wrong with the world and dwelt on human failings, whether it was our leaders or the man on the street.

Fortunately, that's changing. There is a growing school of parental training and business management development programs that focus on our strengths, re-enforcing the positive things we do instead of beating us up for our weaknesses or mistakes.

Everyone has been doing this in China for more than 2,500 years. It began with Confucius and is called face, respect for the other person.

When I first landed in China, everyone I met said nice things about my country and me. They said only nice things. Being in my judgmental, distrusting mode, I doubted their sincerity, wondered what they wanted, and was curious what they said about me behind my back.

It wasn't just me. It seemed that everything they said about anyone or anything was positive, rosy, cheering, complimentary, always extolling everyone's virtue. I kept waiting for the other shoe to drop.

It never did.

I had heard about face, but with my prejudicial attitude, I deemed it a cultural excuse for not telling the truth

Back home, as a husband, parent, manager, I didn't want to follow the example of my parents or previous bosses. I was a student of the D.I.S.C. Behavior Profile System, recognizing each individual's strengths and weaknesses. There was a management choice: focus on their strengths and not their weaknesses. You can't do both at the same time. When my boss thinks of me and evaluates my performance,

I would like him to focus on my strengths, not my weaknesses.

My strengths are:

- good people skills

- communicate well

- enjoy challenges

- results oriented

- good starter-upper, builder, pioneer

My weaknesses are:

- no administrative skills

ERNIE TADLA - www.odysseychina.net

- terrible with details

- not good at finishing projects

- impatient

- not analytical

When you respect someone, what do you think about them, how do you judge them, what do you focus on, how do you talk to and them, how do you treat them? Do you focus on their strengths or their weaknesses?

Generally, the only time we think and talk about people's strengths is at their funeral. The rest of the time, we dwell on their warts.

The Chinese don't wait until you are dead to talk, think and be nice to you. They do it while you are alive, to your face, behind your back, to others about you.

Face, respect for the other person, is the most significant fact of Chinese family life, business, and government. It is central to everything Chinese. Its foundation comes from the Confucian code of how people are to behave toward others. He dealt with it at five different levels:

- subject to ruler

- parent to child

- elder to younger

- husband to wife

- elder and junior friends

Face is showing respect to the other person, which means you must be sensitive to the other person's needs and not your own. You speak highly of them to their face and openly to others about them. You focus on, recognize and talk about their strengths and what is good, honorable, special, and positive about them. Not just to their face but also behind their back.

You never:

- disagree with

- argue with

- contradict

- poke fun at

- joke about

- ridicule

- correct

- discipline

- embarrass

- be critical of another person

If you do any of these you and they would lose face.

Let's take a look at face on a national scale. Chairman Mao Zedong's embalmed body lies in a mausoleum on Tiananmen Square and a huge poster of him hangs at the main gate. His portrait is on all Chinese paper money. A statue can be found in every town and city. Each year, millions of people visit sites where he spent his childhood and every place he ever lived. He has much face in China.

There is a biography about him that's banned in China. Mao: The Unknown Story was written by Jung Chang, whose own family suffered under his rule, and her husband, Jon Halliday, who spent ten years going through previously untapped archives and interviewed hundreds of people close to Mao. The massively researched biography portrays a man who was amoral, repellent, and a mass murderer who makes Hitler and Stalin look like choirboys.

- 38 million people died of starvation while he shipped rice and wheat to Russia in exchange for military equipment.

- Millions were killed during his Cultural Revolution and millions of others ruined.

- He was responsible for 70 million deaths.

In China, Mao is a hero, an extreme example of face on a national level.

With face, there is really never any need for forgiveness. They never judge. They just look the other way. Mistakes are natural occurrences for us humans, so why beat ourselves up over it. What does rubbing our noses in it accomplish? They'd rather focus on the good we do, and believe we will learn from our mistakes and not repeat them. They have a positive view of human nature and believe that we are basically good, kind and well meaning.

Over here, when you chastise, embarrass or punish a child or employee, does that mean they won't do it again? Does it enhance the relationship?

I made my share of faux pas in China, but I was accepted just as I was. This strengthened my resolve to not repeat my errors, to do better, to maintain my self-image and confidence, and feel good about myself. The better you feel about yourself, the better job you do.

Confucius says:

> "The nobler sort of man emphasizes the good qualities in others, and does not accentuate the bad. The inferior does the reverse."

That's face!

LESSON FIVE
GUANXI: Trust me

Nothing happens in China without guanxi (guan she), the foundation upon which everything is accomplished. Guanxi is a relationship of trust that includes patience, humility and reciprocity.

A typical business deal in the West involves a meeting with the two parties and their lawyers and hammering out a contract quickly. You sign it, and leave. Any problems? See you in court! I have a plane to catch. Quick, efficient, to the point, let's get on with the show. Next!

The Chinese look at a business deal as a win-win, mutual benefit, and a long-term relationship. This is possible only with trust, which takes time to build and establish. Trust is a feeling you have about someone. You don't put a time date on trust. "I will trust you in four days, four weeks, four months."

Trust is the operative word. They know there will be problems, but if we trust each other and we are looking at the long term, we will work it out. No need for lawyers. No need to "see you in court."

Building trust there is the same as here. It takes time and repeated meetings. Hence, many visits to China, many meetings, many banquets. Most Western business people are not open to such steps and unfortunately spend and waste much more in time, energy, frustration, money and lost opportunities in delays.

As mentioned earlier, U.S. Treasury Secretary, Henry Paulson visited China over 70 times while chairman of Goldman Sachs. He has excellent guanxi with the current Chinese leadership.

An example of no results due to a lack of guanxi from the province of British Columbia. Excerpted from The Daily Courier in Kelowna, B.C.:

> *"Minister Visiting China to Improve Tourism Status.*
>
> (Vancouver CP) — Senior B.C. cabinet minister Colin Hansen says he'll press Chinese officials to speed up the process to list Canada as an approved tourist destination. Hansen says he doesn't know why it's taking so long to gain the coveted designation which many believe will unlock the gates to a tourist gold mine. "I wish we could be making progress faster," Hansen said.
>
> Canada began approved-destination talks with China in 1999, but the process has dragged on. The EU won approved-destination in 2004, less than a year after its negotiations began."

First, don't "press" Chinese officials. Pressing them makes them lose face, which will cause further delays and might mean you won't get approval. They don't need you. Millions of Chinese tourists have the whole world to see. They don't need to come to British Columbia!

Second, you can't "speed up" guanxi and the building of trust. I would guess this was Hansen's first visit to China regarding this matter and he was going in typical Western mode to kick some Chinese ass.

Third, Hansen doesn't "understand why it's taking so long" because he doesn't understand guanxi.

Fourth, make progress faster? Hansen, not his assistant, must make four, five or six trips to build trust. The Chinese establish trust with the individual not the organization.

The EU has guanxi. The B.C. government does not. It is as simple as that.

The B.C. government did not invest in guanxi for two reasons.

1. It didn't understand the Chinese business culture.

2. It wasn't prepared to invest the dollars and time to develop guanxi. Now what money and time did they save? Or look at the millions of lost tourism dollars for B.C. that could have started six years ago, one year after they began negotiating, like the EU did.

One important fact. Any company wanting to do mega, long-term business in China must send its top man over to develop guanxi. This has to occur not only with the top man in the Chinese company, but also with the proper governmental person. This shows face and is an indication of your respect and seriousness and how your company views the China business relationship.

Guanxi is not a stand-alone concept. It is a powerful and effective tactic only with the proper identification of who to begin developing guanxi with. I have witnessed much frustration, wasted time, and delays with financial anguish because the concept was right, but with the wrong person.

For a nation of 1.3 billion people, it is amazing how interwoven and connected everyone is. The Chinese are the originators of business networking, which develops with guanxi.

The key strategy is to find and work with a consultant who has already established guanxi with a broad spectrum of business contacts and networks. He can easily and quickly locate the right Chinese person who knows where to go, who to ask and what to ask. They will more easily accept you if you come highly recommended from one of their own race, which they trust and respect. Initially, they do not trust "foreign devils."

Remember that the Chinese respect long-term relationships. That is why their school classmate networks are so powerful and pervasive.

Friendships and relationships that were formed in school will continue to hold and bind through the years. They all started in the same class and course, but upon graduation, they spread out throughout different industries and areas of government and after years are now at various levels of power and authority. These bonds of respect are still maintained and are indeed very strong.

Here is an example of how guanxi really works:

First, the players.

- First Automotive Works (FAW), the largest automotive manufacturer in China, is government owned and based in the city of Changchun in Northeastern China. It has twenty-five wholly owned subsidiaries and controlling interest in twenty partially owned subsidiaries — including with Volkswagen and Toyota — with over 132,400 employees.

- Volkswagen AG entered into a joint-venture partnership with FAW in 1991. China is the only place in the globe where VW does not own 100 per cent of its facilities. When I arrived in China in 1999, VW had 52 per cent of the automotive market through its two joint-venture partners, FAW and GM.

FAW/VW is the joint-venture company with FAW owning 60 per cent, VW owning 30 per cent, and Audi (owned by VW) owning 10 per cent.

- Ogilvy & Mather (O & M), Saatchi & Saatchi, and Grey Worldwide are 4A advertising agencies. 4A agencies are global and handle global accounts and are owned by three or four large advertising global giants. Grey was VW's global agency.

- Dynamic Marketing Group (DMG) is an independent American entrepreneur owned agency specializing in the China market.

Peter Xiao, one of the Chinese partners of DMG, was from Changchun.

His family was well connected and respected in high places.

His father was a high-ranking Army official and some of his school classmates were FAW senior managers.

In the mid-90s, Dan Mintz had started his film production company, Pacesetter Pictures International (PPI) on his living room table in Beijing and was producing TV commercials for 4A advertising agencies. The 4A agency DDB was doing the advertising for FAW/VW and PPI was doing the TV commercials.

The other partner in DMG was Wu Bing, a very efficient Chinese lady who got things done right and had earned the total respect FAW.

There was guanxi with FAW, Peter, Wu Bing, and Dan that went back to 1993.

Now, fast forward to 2000. PPI has morphed into DMG, a full-fledged advertising agency with the same principals, Dan, Wu Bing and Peter.

A solid, trusting relationship had developed over the years stretching back to Peter's Changchun days, and first-class television commercials that PPI had produced some years earlier. The relationship was maintained by many flights to Changchun, dinners, banquets, meetings, entertaining, favors, and gifts.

The 4A agencies don't have guanxi with the Chinese clients. Every two years, they import a new foreign general manager. Guanxi takes longer to mature and is done on a personal level, not a corporate level.

FAW/VW, which manufactured the highly successful Jetta, was going to introduce the Bora, its first new model in 10 years and was looking for an advertising agency to do the national launch.

Four agencies were invited to pitch for the contract: O&M, Saatchi & Saatchi, Grey and DMG.

The German side favored Grey Worldwide, because it was their global agency. The Chinese favored DMG because they had previously been burned by a couple of 4A agencies, but had nine years of guanxi with the DMG principals. The other two 4As were cannon fodder.

The night before the pitch, our DMG team flew up to Changchun and had dinner with some FAW people including several that were on the selection committee. After dinner, we returned to our hotel room and made a practice pitch presentation to a member of the FAW selection committee. He told us what to take out and what to put in.

Our staff worked throughout the night putting together the new presentation, complete with charts, data, visuals, etc.

Next morning, all four companies presented their pitches.

DMG won the contract.

The concept of guanxi is you want to work with people you know and trust. You want a long-term, win-win relationship with a proven commitment to work together to overcome differences and difficulties.

Since FAW and DMG had a strong, trusting relationship, they wanted to continue working together. So, we showed them what we had and they told us what they wanted. We gave them what they wanted. Western ethics dictates equality to all the suppliers. Chinese ethics are based on the customer. It is the client's money, their product, and they want what they want.

That's how guanxi works!

Business meetings fulfill a different function in China than in the left-brain West. The full bore of face and guanxi takes place before the meeting, where the parties, based on trust and respect for each other, decide what is needed to make a win/win situation. No surprises, no losing face. The actual meeting is more for confirmation, for announcement. We never went into a meeting where we didn't know what the result would be.

LESSON SIX
It's about time

The Chinese have an expansive view of time, seeing themselves as part of the continuum of history with less emphasis on the present. It is only through the passing of time that an individual or business can prove trustworthy. Hence the importance and patience of guanxi. They certainly plan, but it is for the long term.

Westerners — with our day-timers, PDAs, BlackBerrys, to-do lists, and tight scheduling — are often angered and frustrated by their attitude, perception and indifference to "our" time. Our time is linear. Past, Present. Future.

To the Chinese time is circular. When your culture is 5,000 years old, what's the hurry? Everything at the right time.

When I arrived in China, I was so frustrated with their tardiness. They were always late for appointments. Sometimes they didn't show up at all. I perceived them to be sloppy, disorganized and disrespectful of my time. Imagine that, my time.

When I came to understand their time perspective, I realized that what they were doing was more important than what they were yet to do, that at the right time, the next event would take place, naturally.

In my anger and frustration, thinking I was being funny, I would joke to my other Western friends, "You never have to worry about the Chinese taking over the world, they aren't organized enough." Yuk, Yuk! Well, now I am the one who has "lost face" because they are taking over the world.

In the West, time is our enemy. We manage time, save time, make time, and buy time and not waste time. Time is money! Right?

In the East, time is a friend. All things unfold naturally. No need to rush and cut short a meaningful conversation to run to another one. Stay, enjoy. Pay respect to your current audience.

Yes, my conditioning had a powerful hold on me. Even though I knew my Chinese friend would be late, I always showed up 10 minutes early.

Alex Wang, our senior film producer and I often attended various American Chamber of Commerce meetings together. We always arrived early, but it was noticeable how uneasy Alex felt.

As I accepted the Chinese ways, I stopped getting angry if they did not show up on time. I simply carried a book or I brought out my to-do phone list out and did business on my cell phone.

If you are expecting to do successful business in China, you will need to re-adjust your perception of time scheduling and expectations. Things always take much longer than you expect. Everything is always late, by our standards. If they don't trust you, nothing ever gets done. It is all lost in a vacuum of nothingness.

Since I have returned home I muse at how everyone, even in the laid back, relaxed Okanagan, is rushing around, brandishing "busyness" as proof of success and happiness. I wonder?

This I learned in China: get in and stay in the flow. You have time for everything that's important; time is your friend; all things work out at the right time and in the right way.

TIME'S UP!

March, 2001, was approaching and the end of my two-year contract with PPI.

I knew I had done a good job and had done myself out of a job. A good consultant does himself out of a job, right? I knew in my heart there was no need to renew the contract.

However, Lovy and I were not ready to return. We had fallen in love with China — its history, traditions, culture, values, the people, and with Shanghai. We wanted the adventure to continue a bit longer.

Lovy had a robust English translation business going and, as an active, high-profile member of the American Chamber of Commerce-Shanghai, I felt confident I could land another position with a member company, or a similar consulting assignment, particularly now that I had China experience, and was considered local without ex-pat pay and benefit expectations.

So, we decided to leave PPI, but stay on in China.

As destiny would have it, Dan, satisfied with my performance, had ambitious plans for his organization and saw a place for me. He had spun off a fledgling independent advertising communications company, Dynamic Marketing Group (DMG). He invited me to move over to DMG as group general manager in a start-up situation and continue to maintain my training connection with PPI.

This was March, 2001.

In March 2002, it was Lovy's turn. Her time was up! My high-school sweetheart wife of 43 years passed away from a quick, virulent, incurable cancer.

It had been seven years since the kidney transplant had

extended her life and allowed us to be in China together. Actually, the gift of life in the transplanted kidney contained the seed of her death. The anti-rejection drugs she took were immuno-suppressive and left her vulnerable to the marauding cancer cells that are floating around in all our bodies.

The ending began when in November she experienced severe pain in her lower back. We began the customary traipsing from hospital to hospital trying to get a diagnosis and relief from the excruciating pain. We traveled by train to Hangzhou, to a hospital that had an American internist from Loma Linda University in California. He had been monitoring her kidney results and she had developed a rapport and trust with him. We obtained scans, MRI, X-rays, the whole gamut. No answers. No relief.

I used to come home from work and she would meet me with tears in her eyes. She had an odd look as she gently put her hand on my cheek in a way she had never done before. I thought she was in deeper pain or was frightened, but it wasn't about her. She was concerned about who would look after me after she was gone. She intuitively felt that she was leaving. It was then, which I later found out, that she approached our friend, Marjorie, and asked her to keep an eye on me. As December approached, we made plans to return to Canada for Christmas and to get plugged back into our Canadian health-care system.

She was gone within four months. Two months after we returned, she was officially diagnosed with an incurable cancer. The only thing left to do, the oncologist at the Surrey Cancer Center advised, was to make her last days as comfortable as possible. The cancer had spread to her lymph glands, lungs, bones, ovaries, and throughout her entire body.

I was with her for the last four months and stayed with her 24/7 in her hospice room at the Mission Hospital. She was heavily drugged on morphine, but had moments of lucidity and consciousness as the pain and painkiller fought each other for control. In those precious moments, while I lay on the hospital bed with her in my arms, we shared unbelievable moments of love. Those four months and those nineteen days that we were together were so bittersweet. When you get married, they say, "And they lived happily ever after." Well, that's a crock. Every love story ends in tragedy because one always dies first and leaves the other behind.

Those three years together in China were the happiest years of our forty-three years of marriage. We grew so much closer and enjoyed a new life and awakening.

Eight months later, in November 2002, I was diagnosed with prostate cancer that had metastasized to my lungs.

Then, I was flooded with anger, fear, pain, and resentment at the big cheat the Universe had handed me. First, Lovy, now me. I hit bottom. In my anguish one night I called out, "Why me?"

The voice inside my head asked, "Ernie, what do you believe?"

I pondered that for a moment.

- I believe that life is change. Change is constant, therefore it is natural and, if natural, it must be good. Right now, my life is changing, so this must be good.

- I believe in a perfect Universe, an intelligent universe governed by natural and spiritual laws: the law of cause and effect and the law of sowing and reaping. Death is as natural as birth. The Universe unfolds, maybe not according to my plans, preference or timing, but nevertheless it unfolds, as it should, as it does.

• I believe that we are born with a purpose. Life isn't about earning and spending. We are here for a mission, a purpose.

"That's what I believe."

I found that a worthwhile exercise and it gave me peace, meaning and purpose during that painful time in my life and still does today.

My life was changing. All is well. Lovy completed her purpose and moved on. Mine was not completed and I must stay a little longer.

I was cured, healed and free from all cancer both in my prostate and my lungs within three months, and remain free to this day.

Why did she leave and not me? When we finish our purpose, we move on. Just like a good student or good employee, you don't keep them in the same grade or job forever.

Lovy had completed her purpose and got promoted. I am still here because I have not completed mine. I still have much to do. I'm a slow learner.

Part of my purpose, I believe, is to do exactly what I am doing right now — telling and writing my story about China to bring understanding and acceptance of this wonderful country and beautiful people. This is my contribution to world peace.

When I returned to Shanghai, I shared my story with the entire staff and everyone I met. I was the featured speaker at the company Christmas party with over 100 staff. I got cancer and was cured to demonstrate a miracle. It was not a movie they saw or book they read. I was standing in their midst. Here was an ordinary person who worked and walked among them. If it happened to me, it could happen to them. Miracles only happen to people who believe in them. I urged them to have a dream and believe in it.

I have left seeds like that all over China, including with my street beggar, Boa Hai, and I am now planting seeds by writing this book, making speeches and in private conversation with whomever is interested in life, living, peace, happiness with the Chinese. This is my mission, my purpose.

LESSON SEVEN
Communication Chinese Style

Communication in any society, culture, organization, family, or relationship is always a key factor. Most conflicts could be avoided with good communication.

Communication is simply that the receiver hears and understands the message from the sender.

I had always considered myself a pretty good communicator, until I went to China. I had problems in two areas.

Area number one: Conversation. It seemed that conversations went on and on, lots of long, nice talk, fluff as I called it without seeming substance and action. I was used to meeting, greeting, spitting it out, shaking and moving on. The Chinese, and this has to do with face and guanxi, talk it up a lot: about how great you are, and how you look, with many flowery phrases and expressions about everyone and everything. They are social gabbers. Conversation is a wonderful part of their culture and happiness.

Ordering food in a restaurant was a lengthy, gabby affair. The person ordering and the order taker would have a conversation about each item. It was in Chinese so I didn't know if they were discussing which part of China the cucumbers came from, how they were prepared, the appearance, or nutritional value. It just took a long time.

My lack of Chinese conversational skills cost me money in the negotiation ritual at the local market. Whittling the initial asking price down to half or less took an interminable period of talk, back and forth. If they ask 100 RMB for a scarf, following the ritual properly, you can walk away with it for 30 RMB, but you have to play the game.

I would imagine the buyer saying the price was too much because he had a large family staying with him — aunts, uncles, etc. — and that a better price would bring in more customers — his aunts and uncles. The seller probably whined about the size of his family and financial needs, the quality of the product, etc., etc. Through all the palaver, the price kept dropping. With me, with no talk, I had to use my palm calculator or write on my hand and say "no, no" to each proffered price.

Area number two: In business communication with my boss and my staff. Dan had become completely China-ized in the thirteen years he had been there. He was fluent in Mandarin, had adapted to the Chinese way of doing business, had two Chinese partners, and accepted the Chinese culture, traditions and people. He not only spoke Chinese, he thought Chinese.

After our in-frequent meetings, and initially these were training sessions, I would walk away scratching my head and wondering, "Now, what did he really mean? What am I supposed to do? What is he expecting from me?" I was so unclear. I was used to a brief conversation in which my boss would lay out the situation, discuss the solution, the plan of action and results expected, including the time frame. But Dan communicated in a high-context, indirect way.

When I talked to my staff, I told them what they were to do, asked if they understood, (they always said yes) and could they do it (Yes, again). When I checked later, nothing had happened.

I had a communications problem.

When it comes to communicating about communicating, you will come across the concept of low-context, high-context communication. Other descriptive words I use are low-direct-left-brain context and high-indirect-right-brain context. For simplicity, I am going to use the words direct, indirect.

Western people are usually direct communicators who:

- Take things at face value

- Focus on role, not status

- Focus on efficiency and effectiveness

- Direct questions and observations meant for clarity

Eastern, Southern and French people are indirect communicators.

- Body language is more important than what is said

- Identity and status are acknowledged

- Saving face is paramount

- Building relationship is more important than results

The Chinese make significant use of nonverbal communication, such as implied, hidden, nonverbal cues, indirect statements and symbols. They will always quote or introduce a famous quote or proverb. Their speaking is enriched by imagery and tidbits from their ancient wisdom. It definitely has right-brain flair to it. Their communication comes from a thread of long history of close families and interpersonal relations. It assumes a shared understanding between communicants. There are hidden meanings and implied assumptions

The emphasis is for the purpose of guanxi based on the trust and understanding, acceptance of long-term relationships coupled with the importance of face and social harmony. The effort is to save face, to not offend another person and to not upset the order of things.

For instance, Chinese people will never say no in response to a suggestion or question. They will often suggest instead that the matter be given further study, or another meeting be held. Open-ended questions are common because they don't force a person into a corner like yes-or-no questions do. Rather than valuing directness, the Chinese are more likely to be polite, but vague. A high value is placed on ambiguity and tact.

I had to monitor myself in dealing with the staff, clients and others. Think about it this way. If I am talking to a person and I know they can't or won't say no, I must be careful not to set myself up with expectations that will not, cannot be met. Secondly, in the area of asking permission, if they always answer yes, it's easy to take advantage of them.

I bought a magazine subscription for a Chinese friend in Shanghai. Shortly after, I returned to Canada. We communicate frequently by e-mail and Skype. (Skype is a free internet telephony and video service, www.skype.com) He is part of my China network. He never mentioned the magazine before. Yesterday, in a chat message he said he was reading and enjoying the magazine.

Here is what he was indirectly saying.

I have been receiving renewal notices for the subscription to the

American magazine, which expires next month. The renewal office is in the U.S. and I am unable to send Chinese money to renew. I have no Visa or MasterCard. I enjoy reading the publication. Would you renew it for me?

If you ask a friend, "What time is it?" Here you will get, "10 after 2." In China, they will answer, "Maybe it's between 2 and 2:30."

Or ask, "How much did you pay for that shirt?"

Here you might hear, "I got it for 25 bucks at the Bay." There they will answer, "Maybe between $30 and $40."

Communication Styles Comparison

Low Context/ Direct	*High Context/Indirect*
* private space	* communal space
* do it yourself	* work as a team
* task oriented	* relationship oriented
* tell it like it is	* maintain harmony/ face
* specific, facts	* symbolic, circular
* what is said is	* how it is said
* punctual, on schedule	* what feels right at the time is important

LESSON EIGHT

The two things it takes do successful business in China

An open, flexible mind and a serious commitment.

First: an open and flexible mind. May I introduce my two lady friends?

Some people look at this picture and see a crone. Some people see a young woman. Some people can see both, but not at the same time. They choose the one they will see.

If you are able to see both, you switch from old lady to young lady and are changing your perception, your paradigm shift. Nothing changes on the outside, only on the inside. You can see and understand both sides.

Instead of an old lady and a young lady, we have the Western business style and the Chinese business style. Just as you would expect a Chinese or Japanese business person coming to Canada to operate under our business style, it seems logical, practical and normal that when we go over there we adapt to their style.

If you don't, you won't be successful in China. It's as simple as that.

Do you have an open and flexible mind and are you willing to learn their ways, understand them, appreciate them, accept them and adapt and adopt them into your China business approach? It is your call!

Second: A serious commitment.

Is your interest a matter of curiosity, just doing some "tire kicking?"

What are your feelings about China, the Chinese?

- Where would you like your business to be with China in five years, ten years?

- How solid, specific, and detailed is your plan?

- When do you want be there?

- Why? This should be well articulated.

- What are your expectations?

- How many resources have you budgeted for China?

China is unlike any other market you have entered and been successful in. Remember those awesome numbers: 1.3 billion. 5,000. Compare these two numbers with the numbers in your other markets. You can't. You need a whole new approach, their approach. They aren't going to change their style. So you must change yours. It's their party you want to join.

There are companies that were and are extremely successful and profitable and others that did not, are still not profitable, or have pulled the plug after wasting time, money, energy and opportunity.

Here is a list of things I would recommend:

- Go to China as a tourist. No business. Just experience the place, the sights, the sounds, the smells, the music, the food, and the hustle-bustle of the busy streets. Sure, visit Shanghai, Beijing, Guangzhou, but the real China is not in its international cities, but out in the second and third tier cities, in the countryside.

- It requires a total commitment from the top person in the organization. This is not something you delegate to a middle manager. To develop guanxi, save face and get things done, you will need the approval and support of the top gun, both in the company you want to deal with and the government officials whose approval you will require. Remember that China is a dictatorship, and operates hierarchically, with the top man, often hidden from the fray, granting the final approval. They only respect dealing with your top guy. Others will get the run around. You, the top man, must be prepared to make repeated trips to build guanxi. It might take months, maybe even years. How important is China to the future of your company? You will find shortcuts costly.

- Dedicate a responsible person within your organization here to shepherd this project. You need only show up for shaking hands, giving gifts, getting pictures taken, attending and extending banquets, etc.

- Your dedicated man over there needs to liaison with two Chinese people. One should be a respected, experienced Chinese person in the industry you're in, who knows the ins and outs and has already established guanxi with the proper government officials.

- The other person should be a smart, quick, well-educated, savvy, young Chinese recent graduate, fluent in English and Western expectations. She/he will be your go-fer in the labyrinths of China, dealing at ground level with the day-to-day activities on your behalf.

A major contributor to my success in China was my good fortune to have several young, female assistants to steer me through the shoals of being a foreigner in a strange land.

- Helen in Beijing was so helpful in my first days.

- Vivian was my first assistant in Shanghai and I was her first boss. She now owns a successful re-location business dealing with foreigners. www.chinarelosh.com

- Agatha, who co-trained with me, provided Chinese translation.

- Shirley was very supportive after Lovy's passing and assisted me in my transition.

These were intelligent, sensitive ladies who had a deep interest in English and Western ways. One day, while in a bookstore with Shirley I was surprised to see a book by Ralph Waldo Emerson. She said, "Oh, the transcendentalist!" She had never been out of China. Another day, she used the word omnipotent correctly, but in an off-handed manner. I hadn't even heard a foreigner use that word in China.

They all were most useful in coaching and guiding me in my dealings with Chinese staff, clients and even management and played an important role in my job performance.

Get one to work with your dedicated person over here. Hire a smart Chinese student who is studying over here as an intern.

He/she would be an invaluable asset on this side. Chinese like working with Chinese. They do not trust foreigners.

The questions you have to ask are:

• How open-minded and flexible am I?

• How committed am I and my organization to the China market?

Part III:

Case Studies

A CHINA SUCCESS STORY
Dan Mintz and DMG

www.dmgmedia.com

This is the story of an entrepreneur building a profitable business by beating all the global big guys.

Dan Mintz was born and raised in Brooklyn, and was the youngest person to be accepted into the New York Academy of Performing Arts. He started in the movie business as a student extra in the movie Fame. He went to Los Angeles where he furthered his education and experience in film production and created good connections with some of the major movie studios.

In the early '90s, he went to China to set up a joint venture for a major studio. This was shortly after the Tiananmen Square fiasco and the climate for partnerships with American firms was cold, if not frozen, particularly with the Ministry of Culture, which would have to be involved.

He observed that the 4A advertising agencies doing campaigns for U.S. multinationals sent the film production for the TV commercials to Hong Kong, Taiwan and Singapore because the quality of work in the Chinese production houses was substandard. Film production, like many businesses, consists of hardware (the equipment) and software (the skills to use the equipment). Dan saw an opportunity. He was the software — and it is easy to hire from his LA network contacts — and

114

he could get the hardware. In March 1993, he began Pacesetter Pictures International (PPI) on his apartment dining room table in Beijing.

Thirteen years later — with 450 people in Beijing, Shanghai, Guangzhou, Los Angeles, and New York — PPI had become DMG, an international, independent full-service advertising and communications agency specializing in the greater China region generating more than $100 million US a year.

The big boys — Microsoft, McDonald's, Boeing, GM, and Dell — were all there. They had deep pockets, global operations, pricey lawyers, accounting firms, and consulting firms behind them.

He developed DMG into China's hottest creative, independent agency. He then added an events and public relations firm, ICN, and nailed international global accounts along with a portfolio of high-profile Chinese companies wanting to keep pace with the advertising expertise of their American competitors.

He's a charismatic, creative genius in tune with the Chinese culture. He has never worked for a Western agency, didn't attend college, but with street smarts, talent, an uncanny ability to handle diverse personalities and cultures, earned the respect of the domestic and international advertising world.

How did he beat the global 4A agencies to capture the creative account for Volkswagen-Germany's first Chinese brand campaign in addition to a four-year Olympic marketing assignment for VW, a national sponsor of the 2008 Games in Beijing?

He did it the Chinese Way.

The others, the global hotshot 4A agencies, do business in China the way they do successful business in other countries. They are successful all over the world, but not in China.

Let's break that down.

1. Mintz began with two Chinese partners. DMG chairman Peter Xiao had a deep and wide financial background and connections, tons of guanxi at high levels of the central government and the banking system.

   Wu Bing, VP of DMG, has drive, determination and the operational savvy to get things done quickly in a society of bureaucracy and censorship. She was born in Beijing and at an early age was selected by the government to be trained as a gymnast for international competitions. When she was six, she was sent away to training facilities for grueling national competitive training, and eventually became a coach for international team competition.

   While in Hong Kong, she met martial arts and action movie star Jackie Chan and appeared in movies with him. Dan was doing film production scouting in Hong Kong and met Jackie and Wu Bing.

2. Using the guanxi of Peter and Wu Bing, DMG targeted First Automotive Works (FAW) as the company they wanted to do business with. They made many trips to Changchun, delivering gifts liberally and personally, hosting banquets, developing deep friendships and cultivating relationships with the many Chinese managers, many of who ascended to high positions of authority and decision-making power over the years.

3. The three partners were unyielding in their demands on their staff to provide the highest levels of customer service and to exceed customer expectations. Their demands and expectations caused high turnover, but resulted in corporate relationships that were cemented to last. The true Chinese business objective — mutual benefit, win-win, and long-term relationships — was met with dedicated, committed staff.

An Outstanding Successful Advertising Executive In North America, Not In China

The Bora was the most successful new car in China and FAW/VW couldn't make them fast enough.

The Germans, still hurting over not getting their advertising agency, were really smarting because DMG was not following their global policy for advertising and marketing style and format. Yet, sales were phenomenal. VW hired a world-class market research Hong Kong firm to investigate the reason for the amazing launch results.

The conclusion: although DMG didn't follow the global VW policy, the market place responded because the Chinese react to someone who markets to them the Chinese way.

OK, now for the big one. At a time when global car sales in the rest of the world were going down the tubes, VW decided to introduce the Golf, the No. 1 selling car in the world, to China, the fastest growing car market. The market in China was experiencing 40%-50% annual increases.

This time, VW and FAW asked DMG to do the Golf launch without any competitive bidding.

DMG could see that VW Germany wanted to consolidate its

advertising and marketing in China with a single supervising agency, which it would also use for the 2008 Olympics. VW, which was an Olympics sponsor, was going big time in China and DMG wanted in on the trip.

It was crucial that the Golf launch be as outstanding as the Bora had been. It was viewed as a stepping-stone in Dan's grand plan for his international marketing communications empire. In order to do that, he had to:

- maintain the guanxi of the FAW/DMG relationship

- make the Golf the best selling car in China as it was in the rest of the world

- get on the on-ramp for the selection of the single VW supervising agency, which would include DMG overseeing all the other 4A agencies serving FAW/GM business and the other VW cars being marketed in China

- get on the on-ramp for the selection for the contract for the events and PR management for the VW Olympic campaign

Dan needed an automotive executive with international and new model launch experience.

Dan found his man. He had a solid track record of automotive advertising agency leadership, of successful product launches and was CEO of a leading global 4A agency in North America.

The new man rolled up his sleeves and began producing papers, studies, strategies, marketing plans, etc. He worked hard, diligently, earnestly, and sincerely. He was personable and friendly.

He had also come over with the same set of perceptions and attitudes I had. I spent countless hours working, eating and relaxing with him, encouraging and coaching him to open his mind and accept the Chinese way.

In spite of my efforts, he didn't change and continued thinking, acting and trying to sell cars like he had done in North America.

The Golf launch flopped.

After five months, he returned to North America.

Success has many fathers, but failure is an orphan.

There are several reasons for the Golf flop. In the time between the Bora and Golf launch, the market had drastically changed.

- Several years of annual doubling of car sales had changed the automotive landscape

- Expansion and additional entry of more global players

- Existing manufacturers greatly expanded product variety and selection

- All the more it was necessary that the lead man be thinking and implementing the Chinese way, not the Western way.

DMG continued on, winning the creative account for VW's first Chinese brand campaign over O&M, DDB, BBDO, Grey Global and Saatchi & Saatchi. In addition, VW gave DMG a four-year marketing contract for the 2008 Olympics.

So you ask, why, after the Golf flop, DMG win those two large, prestigious contracts?

Guanxi and face.

If this had happened in North America, the ad agency would

have been fired. But the Chinese way is to take the long view. It is normal and accepted that a business relationship goes through phases, but the Chinese focus on the long-term, on strengths, trust and respect.

They had known and worked with DMG for over ten years. They respected and trusted each other.

MICROSOFT IN CHINA

It took Bill Gates twelve years and billions of missed revenue, profit and market share opportunities to learn how to do business in China ... the Chinese Way.

Microsoft came to China in 1992. Eleven years later, with global revenues of $35 billion US, in China the second largest PC market in the world, Microsoft-China revenue was $300 million, and it was operating at a loss.

Source: Newsweek, Asia edition. June 21/04

Several quotes from the article:

- "..... struggling to turn a profit, the brash American software giant is no longer trying to change China. Instead, China is changing the company."

- "Microsoft started to heed the critics and to embrace China more fully. It is now broadly co-operating, even flying Chinese engineers to Redmond for training."

- "CEO Steve Ballmer has credited his 'very well-connected' China CEO (pirated from Nortel) with improving relations with the leadership in Beijing."

- "Even top Redmond executives are now sounding almost Confucian, certainly more patient than their norm, about profit in China. 'We recognize this is a long journey' said Kevin Johnson, Group VP of Worldwide Sales."

For a current update on Microsoft and China, read *Guanxi (The Art of Relationships): Microsoft, China, and Bill Gates' Plan to Win the Road Ahead,* by Robert Buderi and Gregory T. Huang.

WAL-MART IN CHINA

Wal-Mart came to China in 1996. In a retail market that has a 15 per cent a year annual sales growth, after a decade of fighting the Chinese Way, Wal-Mart has only 3.1 per cent of the market, compared with 60 per cent of the Mexican market. Like Microsoft, it has finally seen the light and is adapting to Chinese consumers customs and culture. Recent changes include:

- acquiring a Taiwanese-owned chain of more than 100 box-stores in 20 provinces in China, for $1 billon, which will still give it only 8.9 per cent of the retail market.

- selling fresh fish, crabs, clams, eels and tortoises. Consumers plunge fishing nets into the serve-yourself, in-store tanks. No dead fish for the Chinese.

- Displaying meat uncovered.

- after eight years of fighting it, Wal-Mart has accepted organized labor and unions in their stores.

- replacing their American chief China executive, a 32-year Wal-Mart veteran from Bentonville, Arkansas, with a Chinese Hong-Kong retailing executive who ran 1,400 stores in Asia and has opened 800 stores since 2001.

Companies like Wal-Mart and Microsoft have deep pockets and other global revenue streams to be able to afford ten- and twelve-year learning curves in China.

My mentor used to say: "The wise man learns from experience. The very wise learn from other people's experience."

From *China Business Culture: Strategies for Success*. Wang, Zhang and Goodfellow.

"Understanding changing business values and the characteristics of the Chinese business culture is a challenging project. It is a process of accepting differences, adapting to change and adopting new ways of of managing across cultures. Unfortunately, for every one cross-culturally viable project that proceeds to the formal stage of business-business negotiations, it is estimated that up to nine out of ten fail because of "misunderstandings. Cultural risk factors have been not taken seriously enough by many businesspeople."

A Summary: Doing Business In China

It consists of understanding, accepting, adapting, adopting, and changing your attitude and behavior policies to encompass these facts:

I invite you to use this list as a check sheet and grade yourself on a scale from 1-10 (with 10 being the highest) to get a quantitative, interactive glimpse of your willingness and your readiness to do business in China.

- Have an open mind. Are you prepared to change your paradigm, not just pay lip service?

- Be mindful of living and working in a culture that is 5,000 years old.

- Become aware of the basic tenets of Confucianism, which influences all things Chinese.

- Truly understand and accept the concepts of face and guanxi as important aspects of doing business in China.

- Change your North American paradigm about time.

- Throw away your to-do lists and tight, action-packed schedules. Understand and go with the Chinese flow.

Cell phones are OK. Everyone uses them, including in most meetings. Somehow answering your cell in a meeting does not hamper respect.

- Learn and understand and negotiate "Chinese style."

- Understand why Chinese people won't say no.

- Know and accept the fact that true negotiation begins after the contract is signed.

- Recognize the power of reciprocity.

- Be aware and alert to the importance of business dining rituals.

- Appreciate that China is a high-context society with a high-context language and communication style.

- After all your hard data, studies, research, market analysis, planning, strategies, etc. what is really needed are the right people. This is not unique to China.

- Be clear and understand the rituals of gift giving, business cards and seating arrangements.

- Honor the importance of hierarchy.

- Understand and respect the values of Chinese family, corporate and cultural traditions: harmony, avoiding conflict, avoiding embarrassing others, enhance and uplift others, respect age, tradition.

- After the lawyers and accountants have presented the perfect business plan and contracts, just before you get on the plane, consider the Chinese business math formula: $2 + 2 = 1/2$. It goes like this:

- o   Time expectation: it will take at least twice as long

- o   Expense budget: it will cost at least twice as much

- o   Expected profit: it will be 1/2 or less as much.

- o   2 + 2 = 1/2.

If you can live with that, go on over.

You're ready for the biggest, most exciting time in business history.

You're ready for China.

EPILOGUE

I interviewed Irv Beiman, PhD, founder and chairman of e-Gate Consulting Shanghai Ltd. Irv, who earned his PhD in psychology from the University of Illinois, has helped more than one hundred companies in North America and Asia improve their performance. He was the first foreign psychologist and organizational development expert to live and work in China.

He founded East Gate Consulting in Shanghai in 1993, obtaining China's first WFOE license for management consulting and development. In 1997, Hewitt Associates bought his firm and he stayed on as country manager with them until 1998. Then, he and his wife retired to Maui. Two years later, they returned to the dynamic throb of business life in Shanghai and founded eGate Consulting Shanghai Co. Ltd. helping global and Chinese companies with strategy, focused organization and a balanced scorecard.

I asked Irv,

"What would you say are the three most common mistakes ex-pat managers make in China?"

Irv's reply:

1. "Unconsciously assuming they can do things in China the way they do them in U.S./Euro.

2. Thinking the Chinese who speak English the best are the best managers or are the brighter/better employees.

3. Thinking the ones who don't speak English are not so smart!"

Then I asked him, "What do the ex-pat managers do that that makes them successful in China?"

Irv replied:

1. "They become aware of all their assumptions, and drop them, because they will be violated.

2. They learn to unpucker, breath and not scream/yell so much when their assumptions prove to be wrong.

3. They are of good/right intention and trustworthy, and the local employees as a result will work very hard for them.

4. They hire the right people initially, and get them involved in hiring the others because foreigners will often make mistakes (and pick the ones who speak English the best and are best at managing up, rather than sideways and down)."

In personal summation, I can say that the seven years I spent in China changed my life forever.

- I had more life experiences in those seven years than the previous sixty-one years of living.

- I broadened my horizons, gained a worldview.

- I gained purpose, meaning and connection.

- I am more open, receptive, accepting, and non-judgmental toward other viewpoints, cultures, persons and organizations.

For those of you who might have harbored doubts, fears, questions about China, it is my purpose, that after reading this book, you will consider changing your mind about China. Read a book, take a course, go there for a holiday, start a business, whatever.

Let's face it, China is in our future.

It's in our face.

Coming Next From Ernie Tadla

The Conversation That Changed My Life: One Man's Spiritual Odyssey.

Review and foreword by Jaret Blidook.

Along the journey of life, we encounter experiences that many people credit to chance. However, there are a few instances where even the staunchest skeptics must give pause and examine the thought,

"Is something larger going on here?" Certain 'coincidences' escape our control, and cause feelings of awareness beyond our view.

Circumstances will touch us with such power and poignancy that one must wonder if there is such a thing as a "Divine Scheme."

As a Licensed Practical Nurse, I was impressed with how Ernie Tadla came in every day to visit his mother at the long-term care home where I worked. Many of our residents did not have this grand attention from their families and friends. He and I also touched base at a local public speaking club called Toastmasters. We built an amiable, professional, nurse-client relationship. Occasionally, we would chat about the weather, the care of his beloved mother, the speaking club, or share a few good jokes.

One day, our encounter was quite distinctive. Ernie dared to initiate a connection with me. Seeming to know that he was treading on thin ice, he spoke in an unconventional and straightforward manner.

"Jaret, are you fulfilling your purpose? What do you really want?

What are you doing here?"

He asked questions and said things you might expect of a salesman or a cultist, but somehow this was different; I could tell that he really cared. As well, many of the things he said were not new, but a confirmation of that which I sort of knew already.

Later, he e-mailed some encouraging words, and lent me a stack of books. 'Coincidentally', several friends and family members had already mentioned a few of the authors and titles. We enjoyed good walks around Shannon Lake, where I poured out some of my doubts, concerns, and fears. Ernie responded with encouragement, faith, and a positive mind.

A former Christian pastor about his belief system. "I write my statement of faith in pencil," he replied, "as it is always changing." While this would be very controversial to those who enjoy everything in nice little packages, his answer reflects a lifetime of studying, questioning, and gaining understanding. So too, I've found these qualities in Ernie.

In The Success Principles, Jack Canfield, co-author of Chicken Soup for the Soul, states, "Believe that the Universe is conspiring to do you good, not harm." For many, this concept is almost too profound, but some grasp the idea and learn that the Creator, the Source, Yahweh, God, is not out to "get them." Canfield gives example after example of people who have embraced a new attitude, and have achieved their dreams. Threaded throughout "Ernie's Conversations," you will find the themes of physical, mental and spiritual success.

Today, I consider Ernie Tadla a confidant, mentor and good friend. He stepped out, made a difference in my life, and dared to be a catalyst for constructive, personal change.

It is refreshing to meet people who don't insist on being "always right," but allow others to agree or disagree and continue to love unconditionally.

Whether Ernie's perceptions within The Conversation That Changed My Life inspire you, challenge your beliefs, or even cause some discomfort, may you find hope, enjoy peace, and become more aware of the Energy that connects us all.

On my fridge door is a quote by Karlene Kerfoot. "Inspirational leaders truly love what they do, and sincerely love and care about the people who work with them ... they unleash potential by inspiring people from within."

Thank you, Ernie, for inspiration, for leadership and for caring.

May your life be an effective, positive influence for many, many people.

Blessings,
Jaret Blidook,
Westbank, B.C.

ISBN 142510120-8